I0605288
THIS BELONGS TO

SHADOW GROWTH JOURNEY

Discover Your Hidden Self

This edition published by Piccadilly (USA) Inc.

10 9 8 7 6 5 4 3 2 1

Made in China

ISBN: 978-1-48897-521-9

MY PLEDGE

I, ______________________________ joyfully pledge on this day to embark on a journey of self-discovery and kindness. I promise to navigate this journal with a spirit of curiosity and gentle honesty. I recognize that I am a tapestry of laughter, tears, strengths, and fears, and I lovingly commit to honoring each thread.

____

Signature

____

Start date

____

Completion date

There is a part of you that lives quietly beneath the surface—unseen, often unspoken, yet always present. It holds your hidden truths, your quiet wounds, your silenced instincts, and the parts of yourself you've learned to set aside. This is your shadow.

In the pages ahead, you'll be gently guided to explore this part of yourself—not to control or fix it, but to understand and integrate it. Shadow growth is a process of meeting what's been buried, forgotten, or pushed away, and discovering how it has shaped your emotions, choices, relationships, and self-image. It's not about becoming someone new. It's about coming home to what's already within you.

Early on, you'll be introduced to the founder of shadow work, Carl Jung, and his teachings that help form the foundation for everything that follows. Through this lens, you'll begin to meet your own shadow with curiosity instead of resistance, seeing it as a companion on the path of growth.

You'll also reconnect with your inner child—the pure, instinctive part of you that remembers how to feel deeply and express freely. This connection often reveals what your younger self needed but never received, offering insight, compassion, and healing.

You'll explore archetypes—those universal roles and patterns that show up in the way you love, protect, rebel, or withdraw. Understanding these can help you recognize inner dynamics, break repeating cycles, and give voice to the parts of you that feel unseen. As emotions surface, you'll be guided in how to hold space for them, process them, and work with them instead of against them. You'll learn grounding techniques and reflective tools to navigate what comes up—gently, and at your own pace.

There is no perfect way to walk this path. You are not expected to have answers before you begin. This space exists to support you—whether you're just becoming aware of your shadow or already deep in your inner work. You'll find clarity through reflection, movement through awareness, and strength in reclaiming the parts of yourself you were never meant to lose.

Take your time. Breathe. Begin when you're ready. Everything you need is already inside you—and this is the space where you'll begin to uncover it.

"The Shadow is
the greatest teacher
for how to come
to the light."

– Ram Dass

PARTS

1 UNDERSTANDING SHADOW WORK

2 INTRODUCTION TO YOUR SHADOW

3 RECONNECTING WITH YOUR INNER CHILD: HEAL YOUR YOUNGER SELF

4 EXPLORING JUNGIAN PSYCHOLOGY & THE LAYERS OF SHADOW WORK

5 UNLEASH YOUR EMOTIONS & EXPRESS YOURSELF

6 GETTING STARTED WITH SHADOW WORK: EXERCISES

7 SELF-CARE PRACTICES TO PARTNER WITH SHADOW WORK

8 FINAL REFLECTION

1

UNDERSTANDING SHADOW WORK

LEARNING FROM CARL JUNG: The Man Who Started It All

Carl Jung, born in 1875, was a pioneering figure in the field of psychology. He was a Swiss psychiatrist and psychoanalyst who founded Jungian psychology, also referred to analytical psychology. He had a knack for understanding the deeper parts of our psyche. He introduced the idea of the 'shadow,' which is like the storeroom of everything we've tucked away over the years – our fears, hidden desires, and unacknowledged parts of our personality.

Carl Jung's shadow work theory is about exploring the hidden or unconscious parts of ourselves, which he called the "shadow." It involves acknowledging and integrating these aspects of our personality that we tend to ignore or suppress. Essentially, it's about facing our fears, insecurities, and darker emotions to achieve a more balanced and whole self. By embracing our shadow, we can better understand ourselves and develop healthier relationships with others.

Jung's core idea suggests getting to know your shadow isn't about getting rid of the bad stuff; it's about understanding and embracing it. He believed that by integrating these hidden parts, we could become more whole and authentic. It's like finding pieces of a puzzle you didn't know were missing and finally seeing the full picture of who you are.

In Jungian psychology, the shadow isn't the only part of our unconscious. Jung also talked about archetypes, which are universal patterns or symbols that exist in the collective unconscious. These archetypes represent common human experiences and emotions, like the Sage, the Caregiver, the Ruler, and many others. Shadow work involves recognizing how these archetypes manifest in our lives and understanding their influence on our behavior and relationships. By exploring our personal archetypes and shadows, we can gain insight into our motivations and develop a deeper understanding of ourselves which leads to personal growth, self-awareness and acceptance.

We will take a deeper dive into the many different layers and aspects of Jung's analytical psychology later in this journal, this is just an overview. Jung didn't see the shadow as just a dark and scary place; he saw it as a treasure trove of potential, creativity, and new beginnings.

While Jung laid the foundation, the true work begins when we turn inward with honesty and compassion. Shadow growth invites us to step into radical self-awareness—not as a one-time event, but as a continuous unfolding. It requires courage to look at ourselves not through the lens of who we should be, but with acceptance of who we are, in all our complexity.

This process also creates space to reflect on the roles we've been playing—often unconsciously. We may find we've become overly identified with certain masks to feel safe, loved, or in control. Meeting the shadow helps peel back those layers, revealing where we've been performing instead of fully living. That awareness alone is powerful.

You may notice certain emotions intensify during this work. Guilt, shame, grief, or even unexpected anger can rise to the surface. These are not signs of regression—they're signs of release. The emotions you've long buried are making their way into the light so they can be processed, not punished. In time, they become guides, showing you where your unmet needs, unspoken boundaries, or forgotten parts reside.

As the work deepens, themes like forgiveness, self-trust, and emotional resilience will emerge. You'll learn how to create safe internal space for discomfort while building practices that regulate your nervous system and restore your inner balance. This growth is not linear. Some days may feel like clarity, others like confusion—but every layer you meet brings you closer to truth.

The chapters ahead will guide you gently through this terrain, inviting you to meet your shadow, not as a threat, but as a teacher.

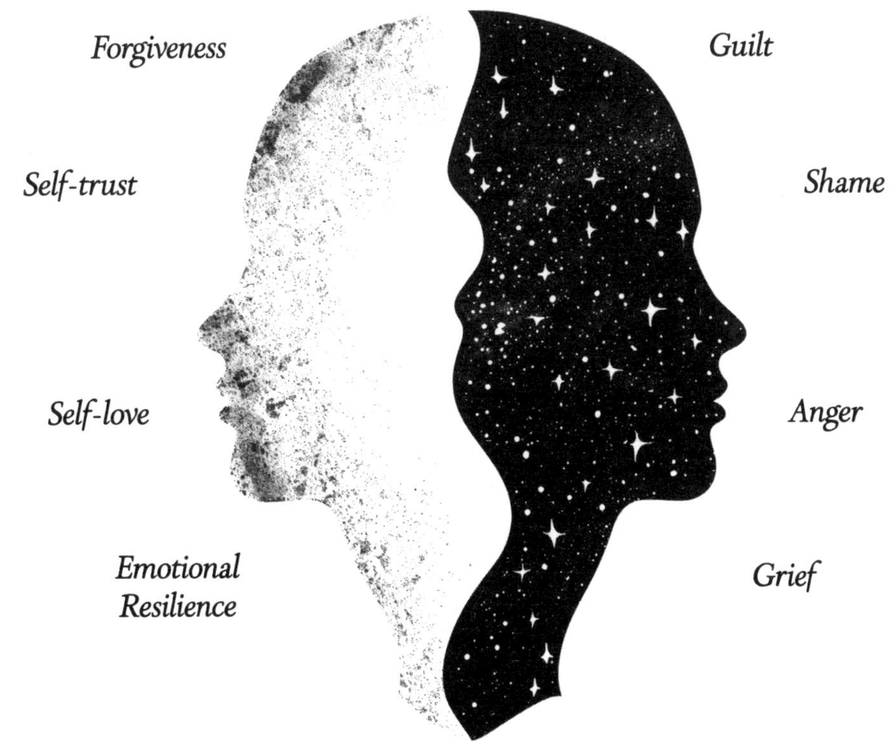

JOURNAL THE MENTOR

You will see writing prompts throughout your shadow work journey. They will serve as crucial checkpoints, allowing you moments for reflection. Additionally, they will give you opportunities you to review what you've discovered and offer you the chance to delve deeper into the various facets that constitute your unique self.

In the following pages, you'll find quotes from Carl Jung. Read each quote as if it were a writing prompt, then write what you interpret his quote to mean. Share your feelings about the quote, discuss its relevance to your life, and reflect on what you can take away from what he said.

☾ "Your vision will become clear only when you can look into your own heart. Who looks outside, dreams; who looks inside, awakes."

☾ "To confront a person with his shadow is to show him his own light."

☾ "There is no coming to consciousness without pain."

☾ "The word 'happy' would lose its meaning if it were not balanced by sadness."

☾ "Knowing your own darkness is the best method for dealing with the darknesses of other people."

☾ "Thinking is difficult, that's why most people judge."

LET THE JOURNEY BEGIN...

As you start your introspective journey it will feel like a scenic route through your entire life. It's about discovering the paths you've walked, the hidden corners you've not yet explored, and the distinctive and quirky facets that make you, uniquely you.

You must be fully committed, dedicated 100% to seeing this through, or else you will not reap the full benefits of the process. Don't give in, don't surrender in your quest to understanding yourself better. You won't want to miss an opportunity to reintroduce yourself to those parts of you that have been suppressed, concealed, or underdeveloped. Self-awareness is the cornerstone of self-acceptance and living the life you're destined to enjoy.

Here are some tips that will help you ease you into your journey gently and also facilitate an overall better experience:

☾ **Create a cozy, safe nook in your favorite spot.** This is where you'll sit and reflect, explore, and sometimes challenge yourself. It's important that this space feels secure and comforting because you'll be delving into thoughts and feelings that might be a bit delicate or even surprising. You can have more than one spot, sometimes a change in scenery is a good thing to bring out your different sides but prioritize privacy and comfort when selecting a location.

☾ **Tools you will need to have at the ready: blank journals or notepads, pens, good lighting, and other items that make you feel grounded.** Having some comforting items like a blanket and pillow, stuffed animal, herbal tea, or stress ball are a good idea to have on hand while you are on this adventure. The idea is to keep an open mind but self-soothe at the same time for maximum benefit.

☾ **Remember that this journey is all about being present with yourself.** Practices like meditation or simply taking deep breaths can help you tune into your thoughts and feelings. It's about learning to listen to the quiet whispers of your heart and the loud declarations of your mind.

☾ **Here's something really important: go at your own pace.** Some days you might feel like you're ready to climb mountains. Other days, you might want to rest and reflect. That's perfectly okay. This journey is yours, and every step you take is a step towards understanding and embracing yourself more fully.

☾ **Lastly, be your own best friend on this journey.** Be kind, be patient, and be open to whatever you might discover. Celebrate your courage to look within and honor every little insight you gain. Remember, it's not about rushing to the finish line; it's about enjoying the journey and discovering the wonderful, complex, and absolutely unique person that is you.

Think of setting out on this journey like you're planning a trip. You wouldn't just hop in the car and drive without knowing your destination, right? In the same way, take a moment to think about what you're hoping to discover and understand about yourself. This doesn't have to be a detailed plan, just a gentle direction or intention that feels right for you.

Now that you've decided to take the plunge, here's what you can expect and what you need to prepare for as you embark on your journey of self-discovery. What questions are you searching for answers to, what reactions do you want to understand better, and what parts of yourself are you most uncomfortable or unfamiliar with and why?

It's often challenging to confront the aspects of ourselves we prefer to ignore, similar to looking in a mirror and disliking or not recognizing the reflection. Engaging in self-discovery may unearth these unlikable and unfamiliar facets of our being. We often shield ourselves from certain truths for various reasons, and yet, our deepest inner richness remains concealed. Embarking on the shadow journey entails a voyage of self-confrontation, demanding courage, honesty, and a commitment to personal growth.

All that we pushed aside during our formative years—traits, attitudes, impulses, and qualities incongruent with our self-image—emerge into the light. Through shadow work, we bring this disowned material into awareness, allowing us to ultimately embrace these traits, impulses, and attributes. By integrating them into our lives, we discover ways to derive benefit from them in our daily existence.

Answer the following pre-shadow work questions. These will help your discovery process and shift you into a curious mindset that will allow you to navigate this journal with intent and purpose. Give each answer thoughtful consideration because it will help you pinpoint specific areas you want to focus on, as well as help you facilitate an introduction to your shadow side.

☾ What emotions do I try to avoid? Why am I afraid to feel them? What do I think will happen by allowing myself to feel these emotions?

☾ How do I show up for others but fall short for myself?

☾ What toxic traits keep reoccurring in my relationships with family, friends or my significant other?

☾ What unresolved traumas or painful memories continue to influence my thoughts, feelings, and actions?

☾ In what ways do I project my own unresolved issues or anger onto others?

☾ What parts of myself do I hide or suppress in order to fit in or avoid rejection?

☾ What fears and insecurities are lurking beneath the surface of my conscious awareness?

☾ Are there parts of myself that I feel ashamed or embarrassed about? Why?

☾ In what ways do I self-sabotage or undermine my own progress or happiness?

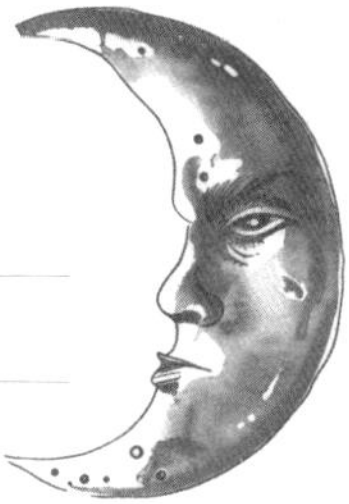

☾ Which aspects of myself do I judge and criticize the most?

☾ What do I constantly lie to myself about? Why do I do that?

WHAT IS SHADOW WORK?

Everyone has a shadow self. The shadow develops in our childhood from our ego as we acclimate to social norms. We learn to change and adapt our behavior in ways that are acceptable in society. However, along the way, we also bury an authentic part of ourselves: our shadow side. The shadow self is formed out of the need to conform to cultural norms and societal expectations, which eventually influences our own judgment of what we believe to be right or wrong. We all enter the world open and free of judgment, but as we grow older, we have experiences that cause us to judge ourselves. Whether from parents, relatives, teachers, or society as a whole, we receive messages about what's acceptable and what's not. Those aspects of us deemed unacceptable are pushed into the shadow.

Carl Jung's concept of shadow work revolves around exploring and integrating the unconscious aspects of one's personality that are often hidden or repressed. Shadow work is the process of getting to know these parts of your inner psyche that you're not currently aware of, and acknowledging and accepting the darker, less desirable aspects of oneself, such as fears, insecurities, and unresolved emotions, in order to achieve wholeness and self-awareness. It's a non-judgmental way of understanding your complexities. The shadow self lives and hides beneath the social mask we wear every day. The idea of shadow work is to bring your dark sides out into the light and learn to accept and love them. But first, you must acknowledge your shadow and then become familiar with it.

Just as a gardener tends to the roots beneath the surface to ensure the beauty of the blooms above, delving into our shadows allows us to unearth deep-seated beliefs, traumas, and patterns that may be holding us back.

Why is Shadow Work Important and Why it Matters...

Shadow work matters because it helps individuals explore and understand their subconscious thoughts, emotions, and behaviors. By confronting and integrating these aspects, people can heal past wounds, overcome self-limiting beliefs, and develop greater self-awareness and emotional resilience. This process often leads to personal growth, improved relationships, and a deeper sense of fulfillment and a pursuit of a more authentic life.

The challenge with our shadow selves lies in the profound and often unnoticed negative influence on our behavior, interactions, and overall life experiences. It's crucial to confront and illuminate our shadows through shadow work; otherwise, unresolved issues will persist, stemming directly from keeping our shadows suppressed. One significant repercussion of our shadows is projection: what we refuse to acknowledge within ourselves, we project onto others, often without realizing it. This unconscious process affects many individuals, causing unseen harm. Other prevalent issues stemming from an unacknowledged shadow include manipulation, outbursts of anger, lust for power, addiction, self-sabotage, as well as manifestations of depression and narcissism.

Think of yourself as a neglected garden. Just as a garden requires tending to both its beautiful flowers and its weeds, so too does the psyche need attention to both its positive traits and its shadow aspects. Ignoring the weeds may lead to them growing out of control and overshadowing the beauty of the garden. Similarly, neglecting the shadow aspects of the psyche can lead to inner turmoil and emotional stagnation. By acknowledging and tending to the weeds, one can create a more balanced and harmonious inner landscape.

My shadow traits: *Benefits to shadow traits:*

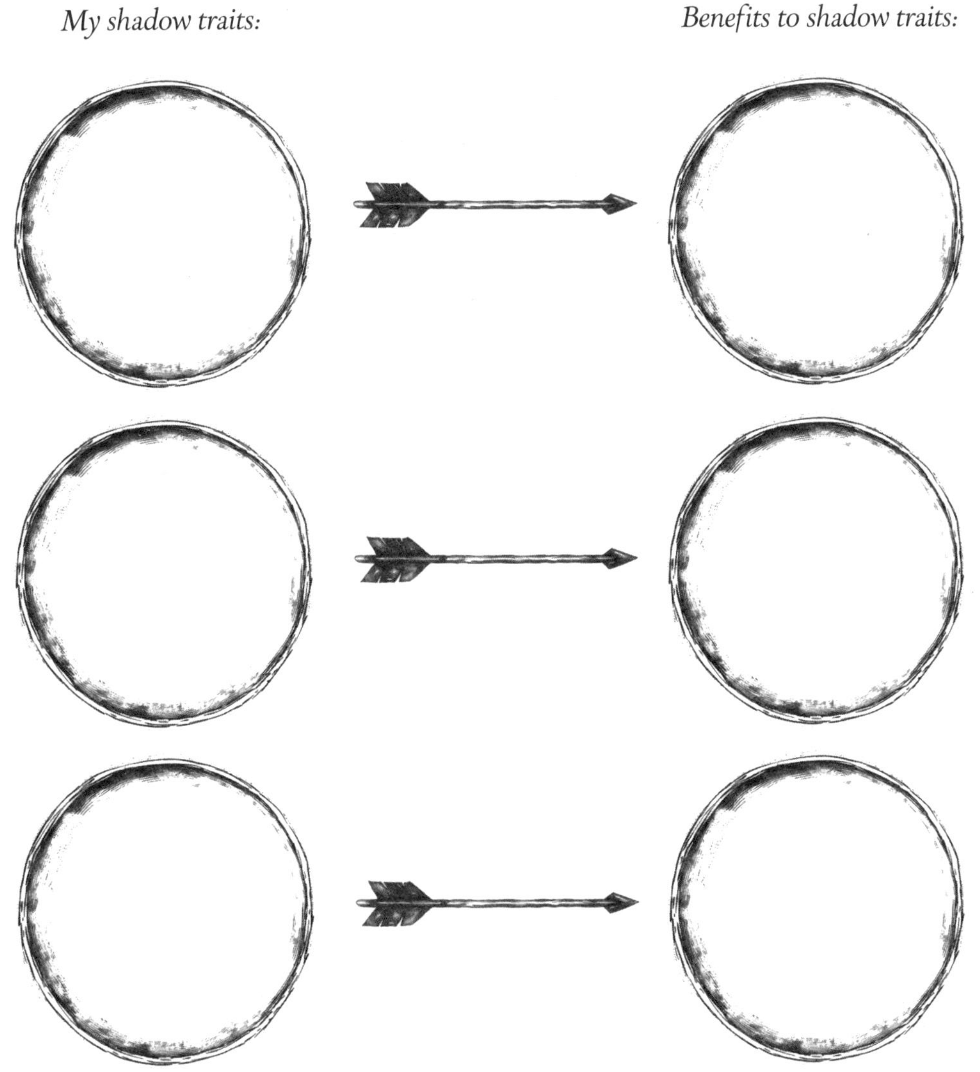

Benefits of Shadow Work

Practicing shadow work yields benefits across all aspects of life. Embracing your shadow enhances confidence and self-esteem by eliminating hidden doubts about yourself. It also builds greater trust in your intuition, allowing you to rely on your gut instincts once more.

Moreover, delving into your shadow facilitates the establishment and maintenance of healthier relationships. Self-awareness, clarity of desires, and the ability to express a full range of emotions make it easier to connect with others. Shadow work empowers us to confront our darkness and transform it into fuel for our personal evolution.

Below is a list of just some potential benefits of shadow work. **Under each benefit, write what improvements or changes you'd like to see in that area of your life.** Identify what's missing, what needs improvement, and how you hope it will change.

✶ *Increased self-awareness:* By delving into the shadow, individuals gain insight into their hidden motivations, fears, and desires, leading to a deeper understanding of themselves.

✶ *Healing of past traumas:* You start to heal old wounds and release emotional baggage.

✶ *Emotional healing:* By confronting and acknowledging repressed emotions and experiences, individuals can heal past wounds and traumas, leading to greater emotional resilience and well-being.

✶ *Personal growth:* Integrating the shadow allows individuals to embrace their whole selves, leading to greater authenticity, creativity, and personal growth.

★ *Improved relationships:* Shadow work can lead to more authentic and fulfilling relationships, as individuals become more aware of their own projections and are better able to relate to others without unconscious biases.

★ *Empathy towards others:* Once we become aware of our own shadows, we can extend this understanding to others. Acknowledge that when someone triggers strong reactions within you, they may be projecting their own shadows onto you. Responding with empathy and compassion breaks the cycle of blame, fostering understanding instead..

★ *Self-reflection:* Allocate moments of introspection to identify the emotions and patterns that emerge during interactions with others. Question why particular behaviors or characteristics trigger such intense reactions within you.

✶ *Embracing discomfort:* Instead of suppressing or denying the emotions that surface, allow yourself to fully experience them. Acknowledge their presence and sit with the discomfort, understanding that it holds valuable insights about your own inner world.

✶ *Acceptance and compassion:* Gain self-acceptance and compassion towards the aspects of yourself that your shadows represent. Realize that we all possess both light and dark elements within us, and by acknowledging them, we can begin integrating them into our conscious awareness.

✶ *Inner peace:* You experience greater inner peace and acceptance as you integrate previously repressed aspects of yourself.

In the following section, you'll be able to assess your feelings about specific areas of your life. This will help highlight things you need to work on throughout your shadow work journey.

Keep in mind that our own insecurities or dissatisfaction with certain aspects of our lives can often project onto others.

For instance, if we're unhappy with our career, relationship, or physical appearance, we might find it difficult to genuinely celebrate others and might even act with malicious intent toward them. It's crucial to reflect on how you feel about different parts of your life so that you can focus on personal growth, allowing yourself to genuinely rejoice in others' successes while appreciating your own journey without comparison.

Please answer the self-evaluation questions in the following diagrams and rate your current level of satisfaction with each area of your life.

✶ *Family Goals & Relationships* ✶

☹ ○ ○ ○ ○ 😐 ○ ○ ○ ○ ☺

Terrible OK Amazing

✶ *Personal Health & Wellness* ✶

☹ ○ ○ ○ ○ 😐 ○ ○ ○ ○ ☺

Terrible OK Amazing

✶ *Career & Education* ✶

☹ ○ ○ ○ ○ 😐 ○ ○ ○ ○ ☺

Terrible OK Amazing

✶ *Mental Health & Wellness* ✶

☹ ○ ○ ○ ○ 😐 ○ ○ ○ ○ ☺

Terrible OK Amazing

✶ *Physical Appearance* ✶

☹ ○ ○ ○ ○ 😐 ○ ○ ○ ○ ☺

Terrible OK Amazing

Pursuing Your Passions

Terrible OK Amazing

Financial Stability

Terrible OK Amazing

Self-esteem & Confidence

Terrible OK Amazing

Setting & Meeting Goals

Terrible OK Amazing

Spirituality

Terrible OK Amazing

Friendships & Inner Circle

Terrible OK Amazing

Creativity & Imagination

Terrible OK Amazing

Making Time for Yourself & Self-Care/ Self-Love

Terrible OK Amazing

What Does Shadow Work Look Like?

As you delve into this shadow journal and persistently engage in independent practice, you'll start to observe subtle transformations, enhancements, and personal growth. Your self-awareness will deepen, allowing you to acknowledge and celebrate your progress. Areas of your life that once caused stress, shame, and fueled insecurities will gradually come under better control as you become less reactive.

As you align with your shadow self and learn to embrace and appreciate it, its power over you diminishes. Below, you'll find indicators of your progress before and after engaging in shadow work, offering insight into your journey's current stage.

BEFORE SHADOW WORK:

- ☾ Running to negative forms of comfort
- ☾ Thinking that somebody owes you something
- ☾ Rejecting help and not being able to receive help
- ☾ Not wanting to forgive others or yourself
- ☾ Constantly justifying yourself & finding excuses
- ☾ Escapisms of all kinds, including addictions
- ☾ Always feeling guilty or always feeling attacked
- ☾ Living in your comfort zone

AFTER SHADOW WORK:

- ☾ Remembering your 'why' when tempted
- ☾ Giving without expectation
- ☾ Opening yourself up to help and learning from others
- ☾ Freeing yourself from negativity by forgiving
- ☾ Taking responsibility for your actions and reactions
- ☾ Self-aware when triggered and choosing to find calmness
- ☾ Giving yourself permission to succeed and stop self-sabotaging
- ☾ Not allowing your pain to project onto other people

☾ Reflecting on the before and after lists above, what speaks to you. What are you most excited about and what scares you? What are you curious about exploring further, and why?

☾ What will be your primary focus for your journey and what is motivating you to invest time and energy into shadow work?

☾ What mental roadblocks do you need to demolish now in order to receive all the benefits shadow work has to offer you?

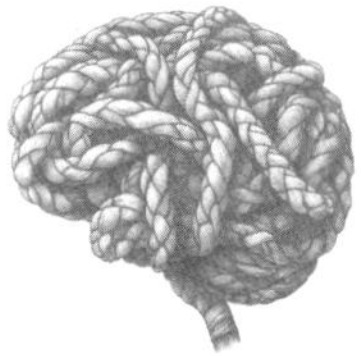

You have reached your first reflection point. You will see these throughout your shadow work journey, and they are an important part of this process. These pauses will guide your path through shadow work, serving as vital checkpoints for contemplation. Reflection is paramount, providing a space to ponder what you've absorbed and discovered about yourself from your experiences.

Think of it as a resting place along the passage of your inner self, offering a chance to pause and integrate your insights into what you've just read and express feelings and thoughts you're having in the moment. These junctures also provide a great stopping point when you're ready for a break.

REFLECTION POINT:
Getting Started with Shadow Work

★ *How do you feel about the "shadow work" concept? What do you think the greatest benefit of delving into Carl Jung's theory will be for your life?*

☾ Reflection Affirmation ☽

Embrace every part of yourself,
for each facet contributes to
your unique brilliance and worth.
You are deserving of love and
acceptance just as you are.

☾ 3 Things I Learned ☽

1.

2.

3.

★ *Key Insights and Takeaways:*

*"Until you make
the unconscious
conscious, it will
direct your life
and you will
call it fate."*

– Carl Jung

2

INTRODUCTION TO YOUR SHADOW

MEET YOUR SHADOW:
What is the Shadow Self?

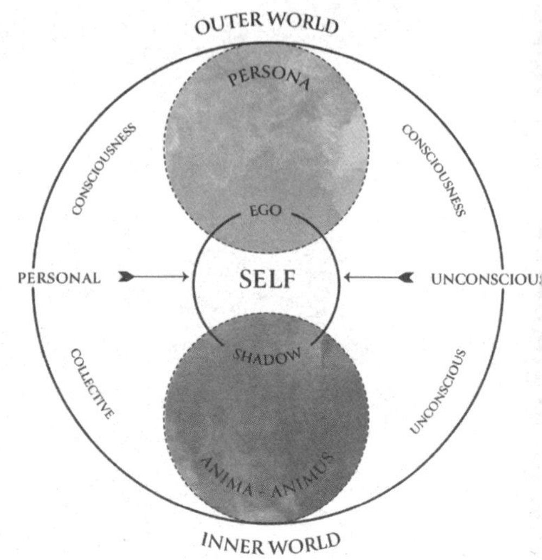

This section will serve as an introduction to your shadow self. If you're new to the shadow work concept you're probably asking yourself what is the "shadow self?"

The shadow self refers to the unconscious aspects of one's personality that are often repressed or denied. It encompasses traits, desires, and emotions that are deemed unacceptable or incompatible with one's self-image. Engaging with the shadow self involves exploring these hidden aspects to achieve wholeness and self-awareness.

Imagine your shadow self as the hidden side of you and there's all these "other" pieces of you deny or suppress. This concept, popularized by Carl Jung, suggests that acknowledging and integrating these aspects can lead to greater self-awareness and personal growth.

Shadow means the unknown or that which we are not familiar, the hidden parts. Jung believed the shadow is like a blind spot that holds repressed thoughts and feelings, not all of which are necessarily negative. He argued that positive traits could also be held in the shadow if those parts of ourselves were invalidated or minimized by others, leading us to subdue them.

Traits like empathy, assertiveness, and sensitivity are not adverse. However, if they don't align with an external preconceived notion of the standard, an individual may think they are inappropriate and suppress them. Because these are the hidden parts of us, they can run around without supervision or operate without conscious oversight. This can lead to an individual resenting having to repress a part of their authentic self to fit in, and then the shadow could manifest as rage, judgmental, jealousy, hatred, greed, or selfishness. It affects every aspect of your life and will often cause you damage and pain.

It's about understanding why you do the things you do, why certain things push your buttons, and how you can be your best, most authentic self. When you start exploring your shadow, you might find all sorts of useful things, like why you're amazing at giving advice but find it hard to take it, or why you're super creative under pressure.

Identify and circle the positive and negative shadow traits from the charts below that resonate with you. Remember, these are feelings, thoughts, and emotions we repress, so they may not be immediately familiar to you.

Feel free to do additional research on other shadow traits. We have left some spaces blank in the chart below so you can write in any traits that are not listed you feel may better represent you.

NEGATIVE SHADOW TRAITS	*POSITIVE SHADOW TRAITS*
Projection, vindictive, denial	Assertiveness, skepticism
insecurity, jealousy, gossipy	independence, adventurousness
arrogance, manipulation, anger	perfectionism, sensitivity, stubbornness
passive-aggressive, martyrdom	curiosity, intensity
cynicism, avoidance, entitlement	rebelliousness, impulsiveness
dependency, impulsiveness, sadism	ambition, cautiousness
defensiveness, victim mentality	introverted, overthinking, vulnerability
narcissism, deceitfulness, paranoia	pessimism, materialistic
masochism, rigidity, laziness	boring, greedy, workaholic
overly critical of others and self	vain, clingy, shy
sensitive to criticism, nervousness	flaky, stingy
judgmental, unstable, hypocritical	

Spot & Recognize Your Shadow

Since your shadow can be hidden or repressed at times, it may not be easy to immediately recognize. We have listed some ways to spot your shadow self below. Place a check mark in the box of shadow traits that seem familiar to you.

- ☐ You project unwanted feelings and traits onto others.
- ☐ You judge and criticize others.
- ☐ You are quick to temper and react to certain situations.
- ☐ You play the victim.
- ☐ You lack boundaries and have a hard time saying no.
- ☐ You have repetitive, addictive behavior.
- ☐ You deny feeling certain emotions.
- ☐ You fail to set healthy boundaries
- ☐ You engage in self-loathing
- ☐ You fail to have healthy relationships
- ☐ You always thinking someone is talking about you
- ☐ You engage in online bullying
- ☐ You get jealous of other's success or happiness
- ☐ You constantly compare you life to someone else's
- ☐ You overly procrastinate
- ☐ You constantly feel anxious or depressed
- ☐ You make excuses constantly and avoid accountability
- ☐ ______________________________
- ☐ ______________________________
- ☐ ______________________________
- ☐ ______________________________
- ☐ ______________________________
- ☐ ______________________________

DRAW YOUR SHADOW: PART 1

Reflect on the insights you've gained about your shadow thus far. Visualize your shadow taking form, not necessarily as a silhouette of yourself, but as an embodiment of the unexplored aspects you're discovering. Contemplate the energy and characteristics that might reside within your shadow. Close your eyes and allow these traits to emerge as you sketch or draw your what you've envisioned. This exercise isn't literal but aims to uncover hidden facets of yourself.

Later, you'll have the opportunity to draw your shadow again, offering an intriguing comparison to observe how the two drawings are similar or different. This will give you a great perspective on how your view of your shadow has changed through shadow work.

THE IMPACT OF THE SHADOW ON DAILY LIFE

On a day-to-day basis, the shadow can impact interactions and decisions in subtle yet significant ways. For example, unresolved feelings of anger or insecurity may surface as passive-aggressive behavior or self-sabotage. This can lead to patterns of behavior that are inexplicable or out of character, such as irrational outbursts, inconsistent attitudes, or unexplained anxieties. Unconscious biases and prejudices can influence how we perceive and interact with others, affecting relationships and opportunities. By becoming more aware of these shadow dynamics, individuals can navigate their daily lives with greater clarity, authenticity, and compassion.

The shadow self, often unseen and unrecognized, profoundly influences our daily behavior and interpersonal interactions. When aspects of our personality are repressed and stored in the shadow, they don't simply disappear; instead, they can surface in unexpected ways. By understanding how the shadow affects our daily lives when left unmanaged, we shed light on undesirable characteristics, enabling us to hold ourselves accountable for our actions.

Take your time and complete the following questions. Think about what you've learned about shadow traits so far and think about times when your daily life was negatively impacted by your own shadow.

☾ How do you recognize the influence of your shadow self on your decision-making process throughout the day?

☾ When do you feel your shadow self emerging most strongly, and how does it affect your interactions with others?

☾ In what ways does your shadow self manifest in your thoughts and emotions, and how does this impact your daily routine?

☾ How do you observe your shadow self influencing your relationships and communication with others?

☾ What triggers bring out your shadow self, and how do you navigate its presence in your daily life?

☾ Reflect on a recent situation where you felt your shadow self taking control. How did you handle it, and what did you learn from the experience?

☾ How do you distinguish between your authentic self and your shadow self in various aspects of your life?

☾ Describe a moment when you noticed your shadow self affecting your mood or behavior. How did you address it, and what insights did you gain?

☾ Explore the ways in which your shadow self may be holding you back from reaching your full potential. How can you work towards integrating and transforming these aspects of yourself?

☾ Reflect on how acknowledging and understanding your shadow self can lead to personal growth and self-awareness in your daily life.

"Create as though you're a kid again, where failure is learning and there's only joy in the process."

– Carl Jung

3

RECONNECTING WITH YOUR INNER CHILD: *Heal Your Younger Self*

THE FORMATIVE YEARS...

The formative years, or the early stages of your childhood, span from birth through 8 years of age, during which you undergo rapid cognitive, social, emotional, and physical development. It's within this period that the foundation of your shadow self is laid. As a child, you entered the world complete, but this sense of wholeness was fleeting. Your shadow self emerged during childhood as a result of interactions with those closest to you.
Everyone possesses a shadow self, which evolves from the ego's adaptation to societal norms and standards. Over time, you suppressed authentic aspects of yourself, leading to internal conflicts known as your shadow side. The undesirable traits were rejected or repressed, forming your shadow. Childhood experiences, particularly those that were painful or traumatic, gave rise to these shadows—parts of yourself you shunned due to discomfort or difficulty in acceptance.

Every child embodies kindness, love, anger, selfishness, and greed, as these emotions are inherent to the human experience. However, as you matured, societal conditioning led to the acceptance of traits associated with "goodness" while rejecting those deemed "bad." Basic human needs such as physiological, safety, security, and belongingness are fundamental and instinctual. Yet, your childhood environment often discouraged certain expressions of yourself. For instance, a tantrum may have elicited parental reprimand, threatening your sense of safety, while playful behavior in a classroom may have led to public shaming, jeopardizing your need for belonging. In navigating these conflicts, you adjusted your behavior to fulfill your basic needs, adapting to the external world's demands.

These were merely mild traumas, common experiences shared by the majority of people as they grow up. However, what about the traumas specific to your story? Those events that hold magnitude in your life and have contributed to your unique shadow. More profound experiences such as divorce, neglect, exposure to violence, and abuse undoubtedly impact your formative years, leading to the development of coping or survival skills that further contribute to your shadow side.

Since our shadow selves are created in our childhood, it's a good idea to get to know and start healing our inner child. The best way to do that is through inner child work. Pay close attention to any experiences or traumas you uncover that may need to be addressed and worked through. Your inner child represents the most innocent, vulnerable part of you — the part that experienced the world with wonder, joy, and sometimes fear or sadness. Connecting with your inner child can lead to profound healing and self-understanding.

INNER CHILD WORK JOURNALING: PART 1

These prompts aim to guide you through the process of exploring your inner child wounds and their connections to shadow aspects of yourself. Take your time with each prompt, allowing yourself to delve deep into your subconscious and uncover insights that can lead to healing and growth.

- Reflect on a time from your childhood when you felt unseen or unheard. How does this memory still affect your sense of worth and validation today?

- Recall a moment when you felt deeply rejected or abandoned. How does this experience influence your relationships and fear of intimacy now?

☾ Imagine your inner child standing before you. What emotions do they carry, and what do they need from you to feel safe and loved?

☾ Think about a pattern of behavior or thought that keeps resurfacing in your life. How might this pattern be connected to unhealed wounds from your past?

☾ Consider a trait or quality in others that triggers a strong reaction in you. How might this reaction be linked to parts of yourself you've disowned or denied?

☾ Visualize your inner child playing joyfully. What activities or experiences bring them the most joy, and how can you integrate more of these into your adult life?

☾ Consider a relationship dynamic that feels unhealthy or imbalanced. How might this dynamic be a reflection of unresolved dynamics with authority figures from your past?

☾ Imagine your inner child expressing their deepest fears and insecurities. How can you show up as a compassionate and nurturing parent to comfort and reassure them?

INNER CHILD WORK JOURNALING: PART 2

Now's the time to embark on a transformative 30-Day Challenge aimed at nurturing your inner child. Dedicate a few moments every day over the next month to engage in journaling sessions focused on revisiting your childhood memories. Approach each daily prompt with introspection, allowing yourself to delve deep into your early experiences and emotions. Rediscover the essence of who you were, reconnecting with the innocence, wonder, and authenticity that characterized your younger self. Through this journey of self-discovery, you'll not only gain insight into your past but also foster a greater sense of understanding and compassion for yourself in the present.

☐ DAY 1

What intrigued or fascinated you as a child?

☐ DAY 2

What did you love daydreaming about when you were young?

☐ DAY 3

What games did you play when you were alone?

☐ DAY 4

Are there any secrets you still hold from childhood?

☐ DAY 5

How would you introduce yourself to your childhood self?

☐ DAY 6

How do you think your inner child would describe you today?

☐ DAY 7

Activity Day:
Do an activity that you loved as a child and still love now.

☐ DAY 8

Make a short list of the things you love about your childhood self.

☐ DAY 9

What do you wish you could tell your childhood self?

☐ DAY 10

Who was your childhood hero? Why do you think they were so significant?

☐ DAY 11

Do you think you saw the world differently as a child compared to now?

☐ DAY 12

Make a short list of the significant things you've made it through so far.

☐ DAY 13

Would your childhood self be proud of who you are today?

☐ DAY 14

Activity Day:
Do an activity that you loved as a child but lost touch with.

☐ DAY 15

What do you think your inner child was most afraid of?

DAY 16

What was something you needed in childhood that you give yourself now?

DAY 17

Are there other things you could be giving yourself now that you're not?

DAY 18

What emotions did you have to hold back as a child?

DAY 19

Why did you hold them back? How can you release them as your present self?

DAY 20

Are there emotions that you still struggle with? How are they connected?

DAY 21

Activity Day:
Try something new today that your inner child would love.

DAY 22

What nurtured you as a child? What nurtures you now?

DAY 23

What does your inner child say when you speak to them?

DAY 24

What values were expected of you while you were growing up?

DAY 25

How are your values different today? Are they?

DAY 26

What beliefs did your childhood self have about themselves, the world, and others?

DAY 27

What is something from your childhood you hold on to even today?

DAY 28

Activity Day:
Do something that helps you to feel safe today.

DAY 29

What is something that you needed to hear as a child that you could say today?

DAY 30

When you talk to yourself today, try to pretend that you're speaking specifically to your inner child. They are still a part of you, and they still deserve love and compassion.

FIN!

Congratulations!

You've spent 30 days prioritizing yourself and your healing. This is hard work, and you should be so proud of yourself.

WOUND MAPPING

When delving into inner child work for shadow work, wound mapping serves as a crucial tool for understanding and navigating the depths of our emotional landscape. Wound mapping involves identifying and exploring the various wounds that our inner child carries, which often stem from childhood experiences and shape our present behaviors and beliefs.

These wounds can manifest in different forms, such as abandonment, neglect, guilt, or trust, each leaving its unique imprint on our psyche. By recognizing and mapping these wounds, we gain insight into the underlying sources of our emotional triggers and patterns, empowering us to heal and integrate these aspects of ourselves.

Below we will delve into introspection, journaling, and guided exercises, that will help you uncover and address these wounds with compassion and self-awareness. Thus, paving the way for profound personal transformation and inner healing.

There are 4 main types of inner child wounds:

Guilt

- ✶ Feeling guilty for not meeting parental expectations
- ✶ Being blamed for a sibling's misbehavior
- ✶ Feeling responsible for parents' conflicts or hardships
- ✶ Feeling guilty for expressing needs or desires

Abandonment

- ✶ Parents divorcing or separating
- ✶ Being sent away to boarding school or foster care
- ✶ Neglectful parenting, such as emotional unavailability
- ✶ Feeling abandoned when parents prioritize work over spending time with the child

Trust

- ✶ Betrayal by a close friend or family member
- ✶ Deception or lying by caregivers
- ✶ Repeated broken promises from parents or authority figures
- ✶ Being taken advantage of or manipulated by others

Rejection

- ✶ Bullying or social exclusion by peers, including racism
- ✶ Not being chosen for sports teams or school activities
- ✶ Feeling unloved or unwanted by parents
- ✶ Being criticized or ridiculed by caregivers

Here are some simple steps to begin your wound mapping process:

- ☾ *Reflection:* Take time for self-reflection and introspection. Recall significant events, experiences, or relationships from your childhood that may have left emotional wounds.
- ☾ *Identify Wounds:* Begin by identifying the different types of wounds that resonate with you, such as abandonment, neglect, guilt, rejection, betrayal, or others. Reflect on how these wounds may have manifested in your life and affected your relationships, behaviors, and beliefs.
- ☾ *Emotional Triggers:* Pay attention to recurring emotional triggers or patterns in your life. These can often point to underlying wounds that need exploration and healing.
- ☾ *Journaling:* Write down your thoughts, feelings, and memories related to each identified wound. Journaling can help clarify your emotions and experiences, making them more tangible and accessible for healing work.

In the space below, write about which wounds you identified with most and why. Be specific about the behaviors and traits you feel represent a moment from your childhood or youth.

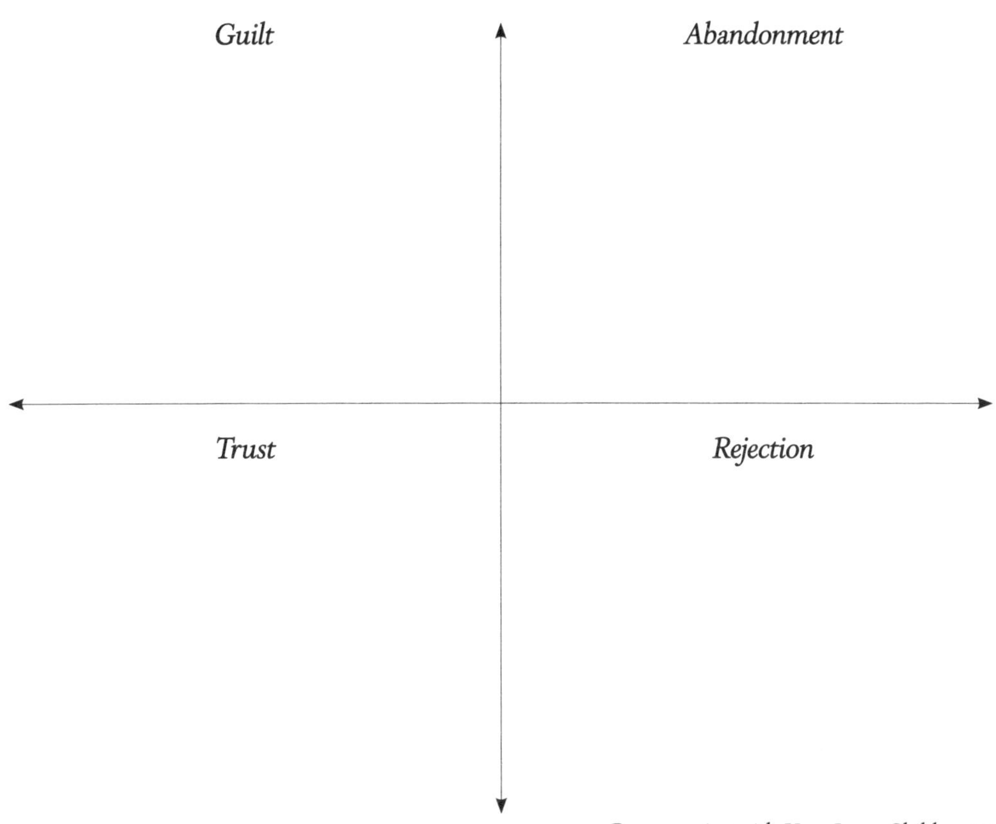

POSITIVE MESSAGES FOR YOUR INNER CHILD: Comforting Words to Heal Your Younger Self

In this journey of shadow work, reconnecting with and comforting your inner child is a powerful step toward healing and growth. So, approach these exercises with a compassionate heart, and let this journal be a space where your younger self feels seen, heard, and loved.

This section should feel like a gentle conversation with your younger self, the child within who may still need reassurance, love, and validation. It's a space to offer comfort and healing words to the parts of you that have been carrying burdens for far too long. Remind your younger self that healing is possible, and it's okay to take it one step at a time.

Let's explore how you can send positive messages to nurture and heal your inner child.

★ *Writing a Letter to Your Younger Self:*

Hello Little Me,

Sincerely,

★ *List of Joys:*

Think back to the things that brought you joy as a child. Create a list of these joys below. Next to each one, write a little note about how you can incorporate these joys into your life now. This reconnects you with the pure happiness of childhood and brings it into your present.

1. ______________________________

2. ______________________________

3. ______________________________

4. ______________________________

5. ______________________________

6. ______________________________

7. ______________________________

8. ______________________________

9. ______________________________

10. ______________________________

After engaging with these activities, reflect on how they made you feel. Did you discover anything new about your younger self? How can you continue to provide support and kindness to your inner child as you move forward? Remember, this is a nurturing process, and each positive message you send to your inner child helps heal and strengthen both of you.

PRACTICE INNER CHILD ART THERAPY

Art as a soul-nurturing instrument needs no apologies because it's subjective. It's a therapeutic tool and a phenomenal way to express yourself. Its soothing effects on mental health have been proven and widely documented. Art is often used in counseling sessions to improve emotional healing, self-awareness, and to facilitate change. This exercise can help you process past traumas and emotions.

Option 1

Here are a couple of way of working with your inner child through art therapy:

- *Simply draw or paint whatever comes to mind without any judgment or expectations.*
- *Let your inner child express themselves freely through colors, shapes, and images.*
- *Visualize your younger self in a particular situation or memory and create an art piece based on that.*
- *Use collage techniques to create a visual representation of your inner child's desires, fears, and needs.*

Remember, the goal is not to create a masterpiece but to connect with your inner child and give them a voice. Allow yourself to let go of any expectations or preconceived notions of what your art should look like. Allow yourself to be vulnerable, expressive and free.

Option 2

For a whimsical journey into your inner child, try these art therapy techniques:

- *Unleash the Untamed Muse:* Splash colors freely on the canvas, guided by your inner child's whimsy, without judgment or expectation.
- *Time Traveler's Canvas:* Close your eyes, recall a childhood memory, and let it unfold on the canvas, exploring past joys and struggles for healing.
- *Collage Chronicles:* Create a patchwork of desires and fears, each piece revealing secrets of your inner child's soul for self discovery.

It's not about creating a masterpiece for galleries but about connecting with your inner child. Feel free to continue your art exploration on other mediums or in a dedicated journal.

Use the blank canvas on the next page to express yourselves using one of the two options listed above.

In this section, you'll find prompts to help you communicate with and nurture this vital part of yourself. Answer the reflection questions in the following pages, take your time, and refamiliarize yourself with your inner child once more.

☾ Reflect on a specific childhood memory that still triggers strong emotions. What happened, and how does it make you feel now?

☾ Describe a time when you felt unsafe or threatened during your childhood. How did you cope with those feelings then, and how do you manage them now?

☾ Explore a significant relationship from your childhood that was affected by trauma. How has it shaped your view of relationships today?

☾ Think about a belief or behavior you developed as a result of childhood trauma. How does it still influence your thoughts and actions?

☾ Recall a moment when you felt misunderstood or neglected as a child. How has that experience impacted your sense of self-worth and belonging?

☾ Consider the ways in which you may have internalized messages about blame or shame from traumatic events in your childhood. How do these beliefs manifest in your life today?

☾ Describe a time when you felt powerless or out of control during your childhood. How does that experience influence your need for control now?

☾ Explore the possibility of forgiveness towards those who may have caused or contributed to your childhood trauma. How does forgiveness or lack thereof impact your healing journey?

REFLECTION POINT: Healing Childhood Trauma

★ *Which exercise in this section did you connect with the most and why? How did it benefit you and what did you learn about any unresolved childhood trauma you may have?*

☾ Reflection Affirmation ☽

I acknowledge the pain of my childhood trauma, but I refuse to let it define me. I am reclaiming my power, finding strength in my journey, and nurturing myself with kindness and self-love as I heal and grow.

☾ 3 Things I Learned ☽

1.

2.

3.

★ *Key Insights and Takeaways:*

"Shadow work is
the path
of the
heart warrior."

- Carl Jung

4

EXPLORING JUNGIAN PSYCHOLOGY & THE LAYERS OF SHADOW WORK

CARL JUNG'S MODEL OF THE HUMAN PSYCHE

Central to Jung's pioneering psychology is his intricate model of the human psyche, offering a comprehensive framework for understanding human consciousness. Venturing beyond the conscious mind, Jung explores the depths of the unconscious to reveal hidden dynamics shaping our thoughts, emotions, and behaviors.

At its core, Jung's model sees the psyche as multi-layered: the conscious, the personal unconscious, and the collective unconscious. The conscious mind, our everyday awareness, represents only a fraction of the psyche, with the personal unconscious holding repressed memories and latent desires.

Within the personal unconscious, Jung identifies archetypal patterns and universal symbols shared by humanity. Yet, it's in the collective unconscious where his model transcends, unveiling archetypal forces inherited from our human ancestry.

Jung's model invites us on a journey of self-discovery, guiding us through the unconscious labyrinth to uncover hidden treasures within.

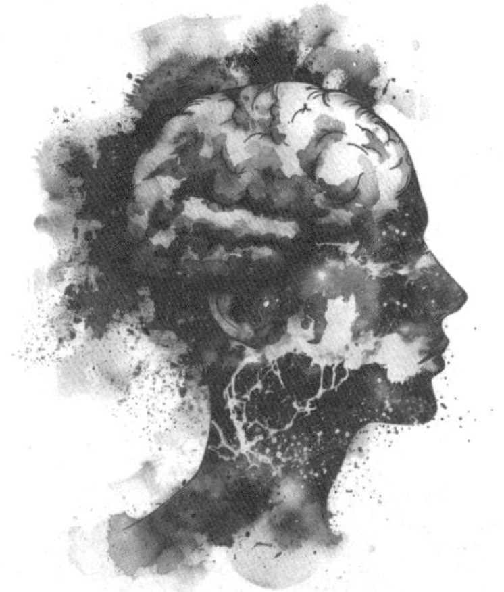

He developed his own theories known as Jungian psychology, also referred to as the analytical theory. Jung divides the human psyche into three distinct components: the ego, the personal unconscious, and the collective unconscious. According to Jung's conceptualization of the psyche, the ego, or conscious mind, is just one component of a broader system that includes the personal unconscious and the collective unconscious.

Ego	*Personal Unconscious*	*Collective Unconscious*	*Archetypes*
↓	↓	↓	↓
This is our conscious mind, the part of us that we're aware of and that interacts with the world.	This contains all the experiences, memories, and emotions that we're not consciously aware of, but still influence our behavior.	Jung believed that there's a deeper layer of the unconscious shared by all humans, containing universal experiences and symbols called archetypes.	These are universal symbols and patterns inherited from our ancestors that influence our thoughts, feelings, and behaviors.

EGO

• Conscious aspect of the psyche
• The center of our conscious awareness and perception of identity
• Navigates our everyday experiences and interactions with the external world

PERSONAL UNCONSCIOUS

• The layer beneath the conscious ego
• Contains memories, emotions, and experiences that are not in current awareness
• Includes repressed or forgotten thoughts and feelings from individual experiences

COMPLEXES

• Emotional patterns formed around particular themes or experiences
• Often tied to significant emotional events or traumas
• Can influence thoughts, feelings, and behaviors, often outside of conscious awareness

COLLECTIVE UNCONSCIOUS

• Shared reservoir of universal, inherited experiences
• Contains archetypes — universal symbols and themes present in myths, dreams, and religions
• Provides a deeper layer of the unconscious common to all humanity

SELF

• Represents the unified center of the psyche
• Aims for wholeness and integration of all aspects of the personality
• Guides the process of individuation: personal growth and self-realization

PERSONA

• The social mask or role individuals present to the world
• Reflects societal expectations and norms
• Can conceal deeper aspects of the personality from others and even oneself

SHADOW

• The hidden or unconscious aspects of the personality
• Contains repressed or denied qualities, often perceived as negative
• Represents the aspects of ourselves we may not want to acknowledge but are essential for growth

ANIMA/ANIMUS

• Anima: the feminine aspect of the male psyche
• Animus: the masculine aspect of the female psyche
• Represents the unconscious opposite gender qualities within individuals
• Can manifest in dreams, fantasies, and interpersonal relationships

INDIVIDUATION

• The process of integrating unconscious aspects into conscious awareness
• Involves embracing and reconciling different parts of the personality
• Aims for a balanced and authentic sense of self
• The unfolding and development of the personality.
• Involves establishing a relationship between the ego and the self.

Individuation, in analytical psychology, refers to the gradual development of a unified personality that incorporates both personal and collective unconscious elements, resolving conflicts such as introverted and extroverted tendencies. Simply put, it's the therapeutic journey toward becoming a psychologically whole individual, where one acknowledges their self-worth, uniqueness, and embraces both conscious and unconscious aspects of themselves.

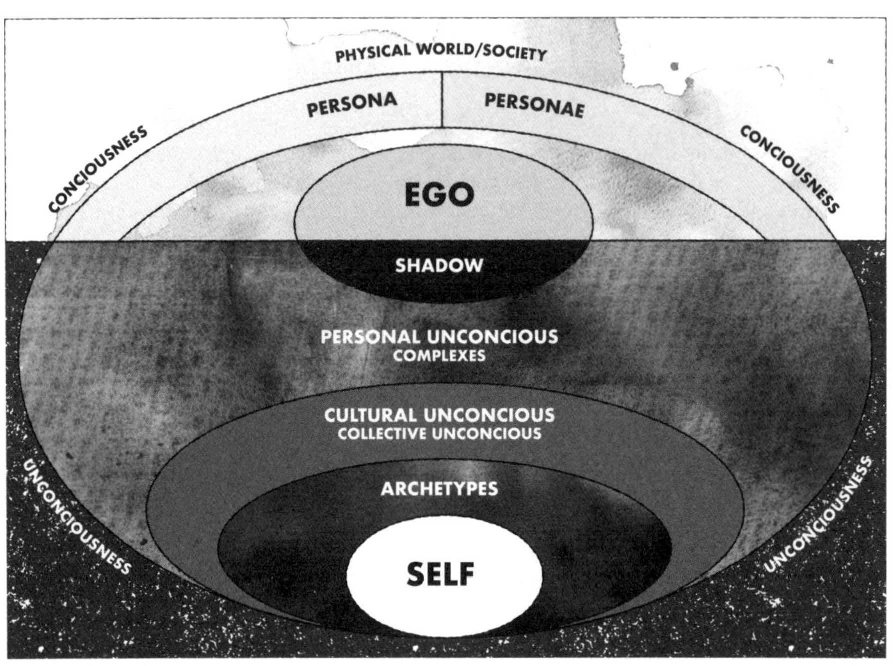

☾ Picture yourself standing at the threshold of your unconscious mind, ready to embark on the transformative journey of individuation outlined by Carl Jung. Explore how you navigate the intricate labyrinth of your inner world, encountering archetypes, shadow aspects, and the quest for integration. Reflect on the significance of each step as you strive towards wholeness and self-realization.

☾ Explore a childhood memory that shaped your sense of identity. How does it reflect your journey towards individuation?

☾ Consider a significant life event or transition. How did it challenge your sense of identity, and what did you learn about yourself through the process of individuation?

☾ Describe a challenge or obstacle you've overcome that forced you to rely on your inner strength and authenticity. How did this experience contribute to your process of individuation?

The 12 Jungian Archetypes

As we journey deeper into the labyrinth of the human psyche, we encounter the 12 Jungian archetypes. Jung believed that each archetype played a role in personality but felt that most people were dominated by one specific archetype. According to Jung, the actual way in which an archetype is expressed or realized depends upon a number of factors, including an individual's cultural influences and uniquely personal experiences.

These archetypes are rooted in Jung's deep exploration of the collective unconscious. They offer profound insights into the universal themes and patterns that shape our thoughts, emotions, and behaviors. Carl Jung's 12 archetypes are fundamental personality types that he believed to be inherent in all human beings. They serve as guides for understanding oneself and others on a deeper level.

Here's a brief explanation of each:

✶ *The Ego Types* ✶

✶ *The Innocent* ✶

Motto: Free to be you and me
Core desire: to get to paradise
Goal: to be happy
Greatest fear: to be punished for doing something bad/wrong
Strategy: to do things right
Weakness: boring for all their naive innocence
Talent: faith and optimism
The Innocent is also known as: The utopian, traditionalist, mystic, saint, romantic, dreamer.

✶ *The Everyman* ✶

Motto: All men and women are created equal
Core desire: connecting with others
Goal: to belong
Greatest fear: to be left out or to stand out from the crowd
Strategy: develop ordinary solid virtues and be down to earth
Weakness: losing one's own self in an effort to blend in
Talent: realism, empathy, lack of pretense
The Everyman is also known as: The person next door, the realist, the working stiff, the solid citizen, the good neighbor.

★ *The Hero* ★

Motto: Where there's a will, there's a way
Core desire: to prove one's worth through courageous acts
Goal: expert mastery in a way that improves the world
Greatest fear: weakness, vulnerability, being a "chicken"
Strategy: to be as strong and competent as possible
Weakness: arrogance, always needing another battle to fight
Talent: competence and courage
The Hero is also known as: The warrior, crusader, rescuer, superhero, the soldier, dragon slayer, the winner and the team player.

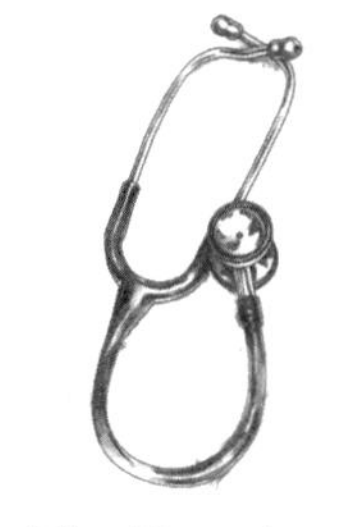

★ *The Caregiver* ★

Motto: Love your neighbor as yourself
Core desire: to protect and care for others
Goal: to help others
Greatest fear: selfishness and ingratitude
Strategy: doing things for others
Weakness: martyrdom and being exploited
Talent: compassion, generosity
The Caregiver is also known as:
The saint, altruist, parent, helper, supporter.

★ *The Explorer* ★

Motto: Don't fence me in
Core desire: the freedom to find yourself by exploring the world
Goal: to experience a better, more authentic, more fulfilling life
Greatest fear: getting trapped, conformity, and inner emptiness
Strategy: seeking out and experiencing new things, journey
Weakness: aimless wandering, becoming a misfit
Talent: autonomy, ambition, being true to one's soul
The Explorer is also known as:
The seeker, iconoclast, wanderer, individualist, pilgrim.

★ *The Rebel* ★

Motto: Rules are made to be broken
Core desire: revenge or revolution
Goal: to overturn what isn't working
Greatest fear: to be powerless or ineffectual
Strategy: disrupt, destroy, or shock
Weakness: crossing over to the dark side, crime
Talent: outrageousness, radical freedom
The Rebel is also known as: The outlaw, revolutionary, wild man/woman, the misfit, or iconoclast.

★ *The Lover* ★

Motto: You're the only one
Core desire: intimacy and experience
Goal: being in a relationship with people, work and their surroundings
Greatest fear: being alone, a wallflower, unwanted, unloved
Strategy: to become more physically and emotionally attractive
Weakness: people-pleasing at the expense of self-identity.
Talent: passion, gratitude, appreciation, and commitment
The Lover is also known as: The partner, friend, intimate, enthusiast, sensualist, spouse, team-builder.

★ *The Creator* ★

Motto: If you can imagine it, it can be done
Core desire: to create things of enduring value
Goal: to realize a vision
Greatest fear: mediocre vision or execution
Strategy: develop artistic control and skill
Weakness: perfectionism, bad solutions
Talent: creativity and imagination
The Creator is also known as: The artist, inventor, innovator, musician, writer or dreamer.

★ *The Self Types* ★

★ *The Jester* ★

Motto: You only live once
Core desire: to live in the moment with full enjoyment
Goal: to have a great time and lighten up the world
Greatest fear: being bored or boring others
Strategy: play, make jokes, be funny
Weakness: frivolity, wasting time
Talent: joy, humor, play
The Jester is also known as:
The fool, trickster, joker, practical joker or comedian.

★ *The Sage* ★

Motto: The truth will set you free
Core desire: to find the truth
Goal: to use intelligence and analysis to understand the world
Greatest fear: being duped, misled-or ignorance
Strategy: seeking out information and knowledge; self-reflection
Weakness: can study details forever and never act
Talent: wisdom, intelligence
The Sage is also known as: The expert, scholar, detective, advisor, thinker, philosopher, academic, researcher, thinker, planner.

★ *The Magician* ★

Motto: I make things happen
Core desire: understanding the fundamental laws of the universe
Goal: to make dreams come true
Greatest fear: unintended negative consequences
Strategy: develop a vision and live by it
Weakness: becoming manipulative
Talent: finding win-win solutions
The Magician is also known as: The visionary, catalyst, inventor, charismatic leader, shaman, healer, medicine man.

★ *The Ruler* ★

Motto: Power isn't everything, it's the only thing
Core desire: control
Goal: create a prosperous, successful family or community
Greatest fear: chaos, being overthrown
Strategy: exercise power
Weakness: being authoritarian, unable to delegate
Talent: responsibility, leadership
The Ruler is also known as: The boss, leader, aristocrat, king, queen, politician, role model, manager or administrator.

Carl Jung's 12 ARCHETYPES are fundamental personality types that he believed to be inherent in all human beings. They serve as guides for understanding oneself and others on a deeper level.

Jung proposed that the inventory of archetypes wasn't rigid; instead, various archetypes could intersect or amalgamate, giving rise to additional ones. These include the father (depicting a strict, commanding figure of authority), the mother (nurturing, unconditional love, and the embodiment of the maternal instinct), and the trickster (representing a manipulator, deceiver, or mischief-maker).

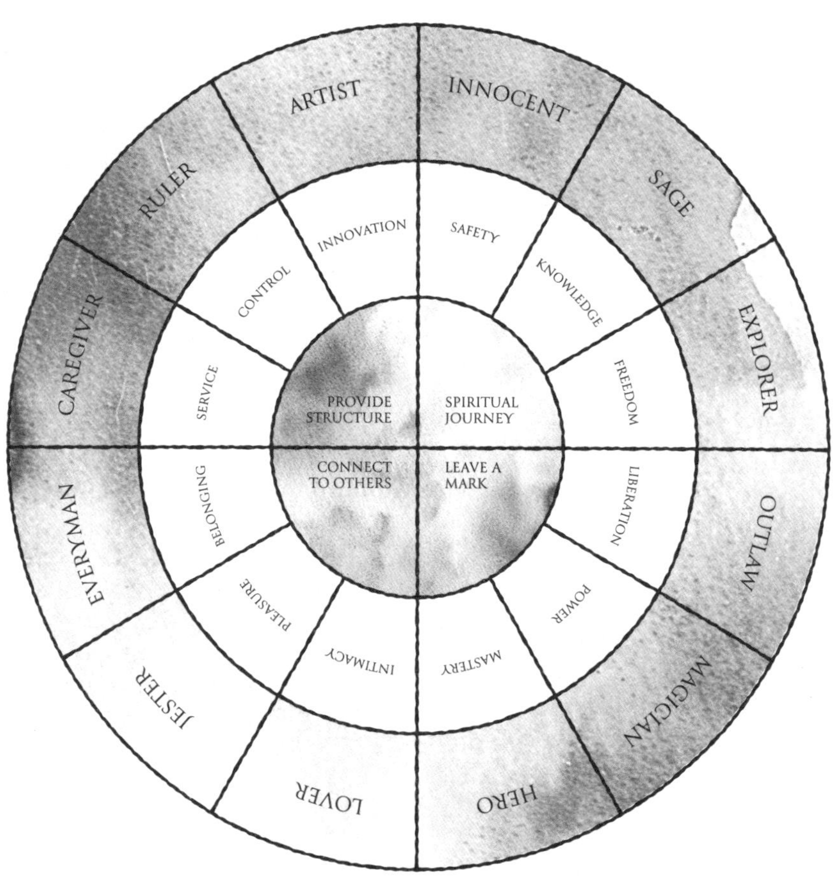

Exploring Archetypes and Diving into Your Shadow

Review the 12 of the main archetypes (remember there are more) and see which ones you relate to the most. What do you see yourself as? What characteristics do you have in common with those archetypes, and did any of the archetypes surprise you? Once you're done reading, fill out the following exercise and put the archetypes in order with #1 being the one you relate to the most and #12 representing you the least. Feel free to research additional archetypes if you don't see one that fits you best and add it to your exercise on the following page.

In the boxes below, write the archetype type and then below it write the traits you relate to the most. Remember, the first box should be the type that represents you best, the one you most identify with, and the last box should be the one that you least connect with.

1 *2* *3* *4*

5 *6* *7* *8*

9 *10* *11* *12*

Shadow Work Journaling Prompts

Use the information, details and descriptions outlined in the prior section to gain a deeper understanding of Carl Jung's shadow work theory as you complete the journaling prompts in the following pages. Consider all the different aspects, the multiple layers and complexities that make up the human psyche. As you absorb the information lean into the details of each component as it relates to you personally.

☾ Reflect on the masks you wear in different areas of your life – at work, with family, among friends. Describe the persona you project to the world in each setting and explore how these masks shape your interactions and sense of identity. Consider how Carl Jung's concept of persona sheds light on the roles you play and the aspects of yourself you choose to reveal or conceal.

☾ Explore the concept of the "anima" or "animus" within yourself. How do you project aspects of the opposite gender onto others, and how does this influence your relationships and self-perception?

☾ Consider the role of rituals, ceremonies, and traditions in connecting individuals to the collective unconsciousness of their communities or cultural heritage.

☾ Reflect on the concept of the "shadow self" and its role in personal and collective transformation. How can acknowledging and integrating your shadow lead to greater wholeness and authenticity?

☾ Reflect on the concept of the "Self" as the unifying center of the psyche, transcending personal and collective unconsciousness. How do you experience moments of self-awareness or spiritual awakening in your life?

☾ Consider the influence of your cultural background on your beliefs and values. How does collective unconsciousness shape your worldview and identity?

☾ Reflect on your journey towards individuation. Describe moments when you've felt a deeper integration of your conscious and unconscious selves. How have you navigated conflicts between different aspects of your personality, such as introversion and extraversion?

☾ Consider the influence of mass media and popular culture on the collective unconsciousness of society. How do shared myths, symbols, and narratives shape social norms and values?

☾ Explore a moment when your ego prevented you from admitting fault or accepting criticism. How did this impact your relationships and personal growth?

☾ Visualize your ego as a protective shield around you. What fears or vulnerabilities is it guarding you from facing?

☾ Describe a moment when you felt a disconnect between your true self and the persona you present to the world. What steps can you take to align these two aspects of yourself?

☾ Explore your relationship with the Shadow archetype. What repressed emotions or desires lurk beneath the surface? How do they manifest in your thoughts and behaviors?

☾ Picture yourself in a room surrounded by mirrors reflecting different aspects of your personality, both light and dark (shadow). Describe what you see in each reflection and explore how these aspects contribute to your understanding of yourself and your interactions with the world.

"One does not become enlightened by imagining figures of light, but by making the darkness conscious."

– Carl Jung

5

UNLEASH YOUR EMOTIONS & EXPRESS YOURSELF

EXAMINING YOUR MOODS & EMOTIONS

This next following four exercises allows you to delve deeper into your emotions and understand your varying moods. All are interactive requiring expression from you. These are personal and should embody your unique traits and feelings.

Draw Your Emotions

Visually express how you feel when you experience different emotions. Complete the head by doodling, sketching, or drawing anything that represents that specific emotion. This is open to your interpretation. For example, if you feel happiness, you may draw flowers blooming or sunshine radiating from the head. Don't worry about artistic skill; this is all about personal expression.

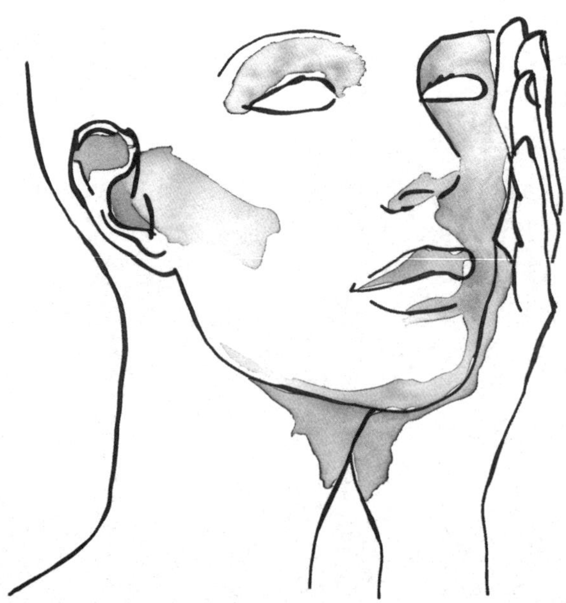

Create a Mood Playlist

Music can echo our emotions in profound ways. Use the blank cassettes to write down songs that resonate with how you're feeling during each specific emotion. This could mark the beginning of a playlist that might evolve into a musical diary of your emotional journey.

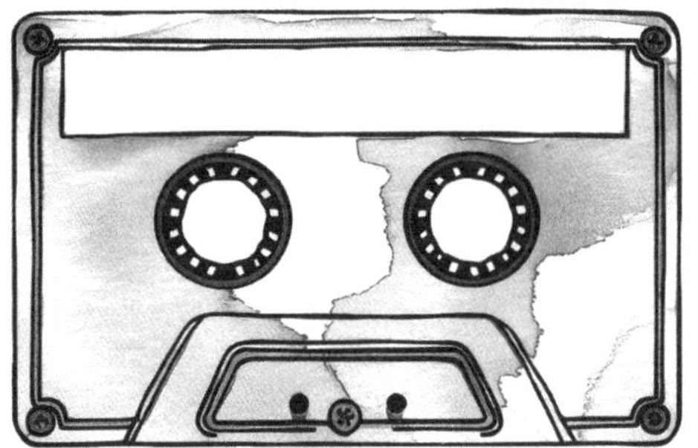
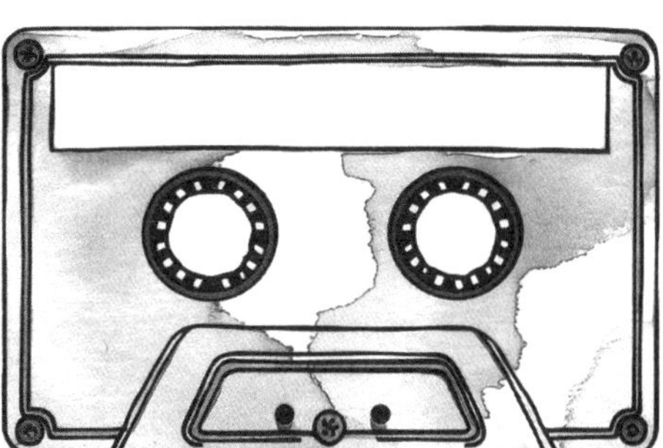
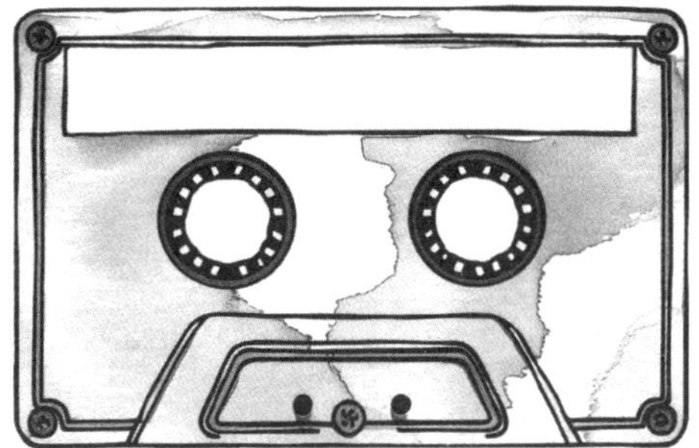
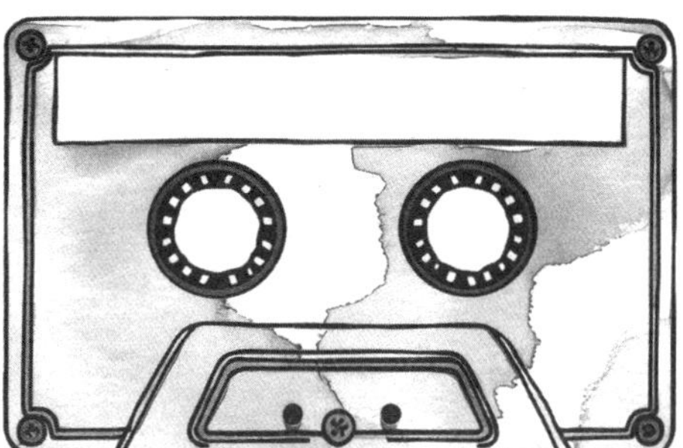
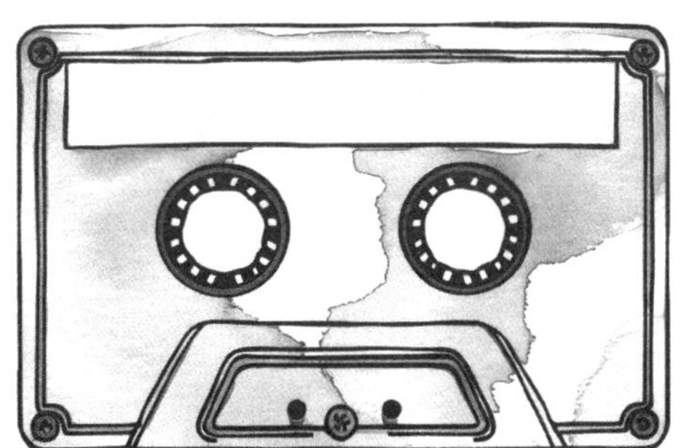
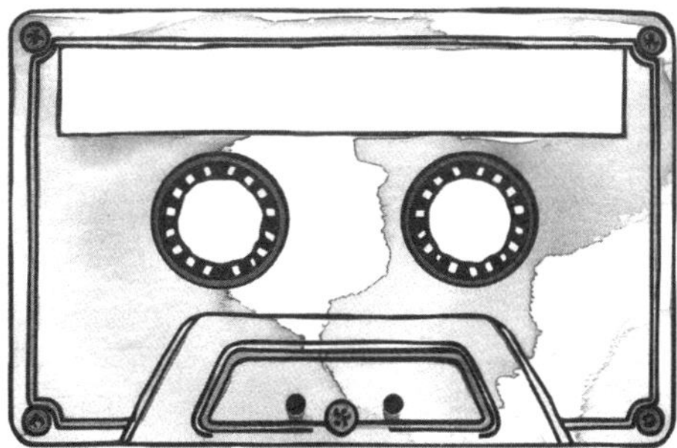

Shades of Emotions

Use the emotion wheel below as a guide for this exercise. Assign a color to the specific emotions featured on the wheel. You can use different shades of the same color for different feelings or moods within that emotion. Everything can be the same solid color, or you can use gradient techniques with darker tones representing deeper or more intense feelings and lighter ones for more subtle emotions.

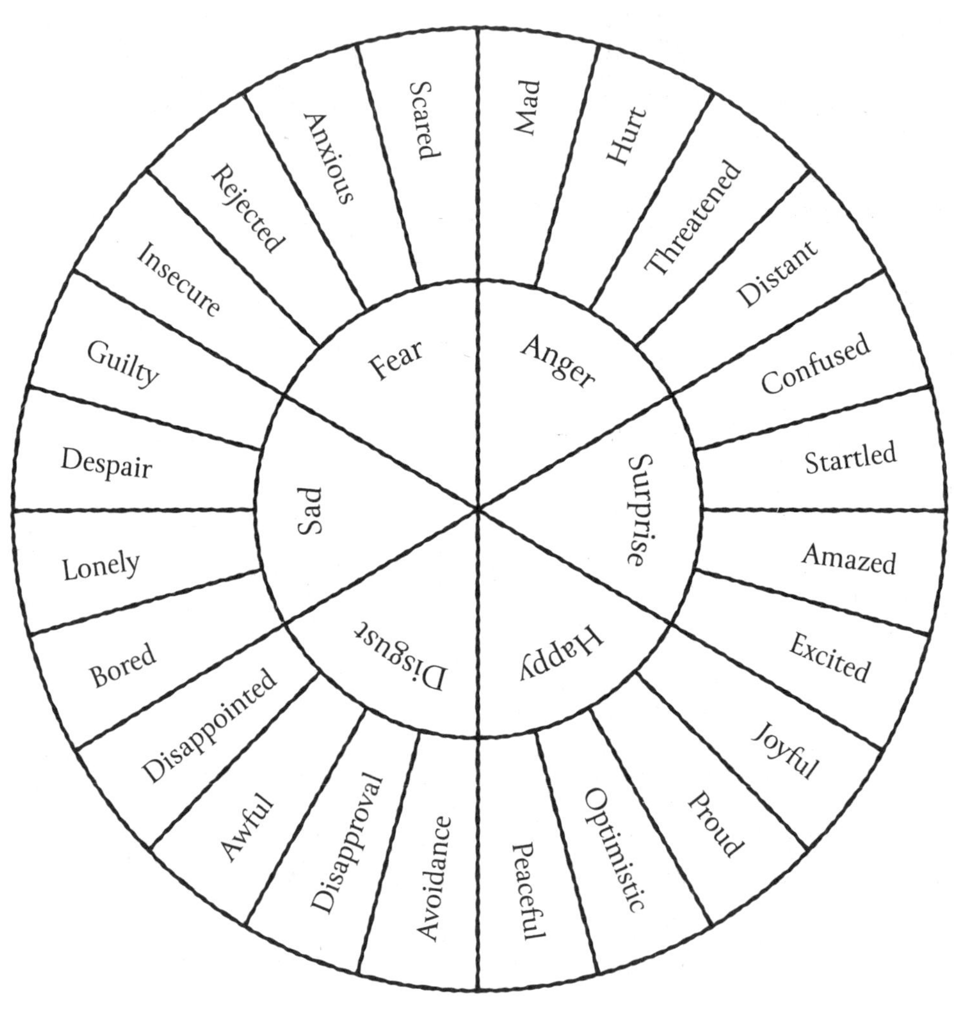

Describe your Emotions

The emotional ladder is a space where you can expand on the different feelings you experience when feeling that emotion. You can write adjectives or phrases that represent how you see yourself or how people have described you.

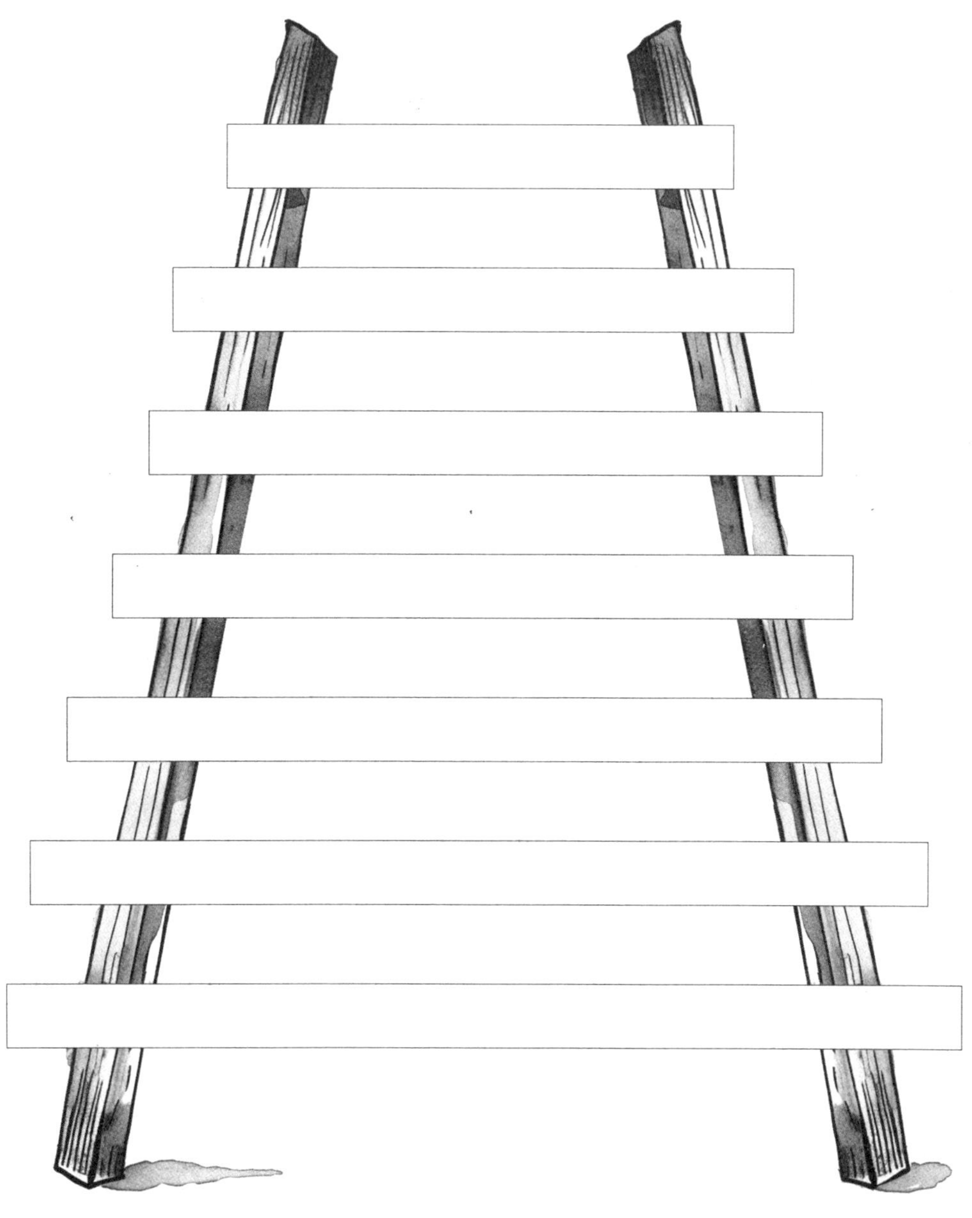

Reflection and Insight

After engaging in these activities, take a moment to reflect. Now, as you look at all 4 components of this exercise as a whole you can see a bigger picture of each emotion. This will allow you to have a better understanding of what you experience, and how you can work through undesirable emotions.

- What did you discover about your emotions? Were there any surprises?

- Did you notice any patterns and if so, what insights did you gain from this exercise?

- Describe why you chose each specific shade for your emotional wheel and what it signifies about your inner state.

☾ What did you notice about the songs you selected for each emotion? For example, if you're sad, do you choose songs that are uplifting or somber songs? What does music do for you when you feel emotional?

☾ When you were describing your emotions were there are moods or adjectives that were represented in more than one emotion? If so, what were they?

☾ What are you taking away from this exercise? Did you learn anything new about yourself?

EMOTIONAL ART INTERPRETATION

Emotional art interpretation involves analyzing artwork from an emotional perspective, focusing on how the artwork evokes feelings and sentiments deep within you. It involves exploring themes, details, composition, and symbolism to understand the emotional impact of the piece. It's about connecting with the artist's intentions and the viewer's own emotions stirred by the artwork.

Below are three different illustrations, each captures the wonder of childhood. They represent the playful and curious spirit we all have in our youth. Study each piece of art, notice the details, allow yourself to feel the mood the art conveys. Take notice of how the art affects you, what emotions it stirs inside and any memories that arise. Where does it transport you to, and how did it move or inspire you? After you study each piece, reflect and answer the questions that follow.

✶ *Art piece #1*

✶ *Art piece #2*

✶ *Art piece #3*

☾ Which piece were you immediately drawn to and why?

☾ Which piece evoked the strongest emotional reaction and why?

☾ Were you inspired by any of the artwork and if so, how?

☾ What emotion did you feel the most throughout this exercise and what do you think that says about you?

☾ Did this bring out any parts of your shadow that warrant further exploration?

WHO AM I REALLY?:
Prompts to Discover More About Yourself

This part of your journal is like a cozy, informal chat with yourself about who you are beneath all the roles and expectations. It's a light-hearted exploration into the depths of your being, with prompts designed to uncover and celebrate the unique, wonderful person you are. So, grab your favorite pen, and let's embark on this journey of self-discovery together!

✶ *The Roles I Play:*

List the different roles you play in your life, like friend, parent, employee, artist, etc. Next to each role, write a few words about how you feel in that role and what it brings out in you. This can reveal how you see yourself and the diversity of your identity.

Roles:	*Thoughts on the role:*

★ *My Hidden Talents and Quirks:*

Think about the talents and quirks that make you, well, you! Write them down, no matter how big or small. Maybe you're great at whistling or have an uncanny ability to remember quotes from movies. These are the little things that add color to your character.

Hidden Talents and Quirks:

1. ______
2. ______
3. ______
4. ______
5. ______
6. ______
7. ______
8. ______
9. ______
10. ______
11. ______
12. ______
13. ______
14. ______
15. ______
16. ______
17. ______
18. ______
19. ______
20. ______
21. ______
22. ______

✶ *The Values That Guide Me:*

Reflect on the values that are important to you and guide your decisions. Write them down and then explore why they matter to you. Understanding your values is like understanding the compass that guides your journey.

✶ *My Favorite Memories:*

Jot down a few of your favorite memories. What makes them special? How do they reflect who you are? Favorite memories can be windows into what brings you joy and fulfillment.

✶ *The Turning Points:*

Identify a few turning points in your life — moments when you felt a shift in your understanding of yourself or your path. Describe these moments and how they've shaped your perception of who you are.

★ *My Ideal Day:*

Describe your ideal day in detail. What would you do, who would you be with, and how would you feel? This can shed light on what you truly desire and enjoy.

★ *Challenges:*

Think about a challenge you've overcome. Reflect on the person you were before facing it and who you've become since conquering it. How do you handle it, and what strengths do you draw upon to navigate through it?

★ *Decisions:*

Imagine yourself facing a major life decision. How do you weigh your options, and what factors influence your choice? What does this decision reveal about your values and priorities? Do you seek guidance from anyone when making these decisions?

✶ *Fears:*

What frightens you the most? What are some ways you could safely expose yourself to this fear?

REFLECTION POINT: Expression of Emotions

★ *Use analogies to describe each of your emotions and how you appreciate each one individually as they contribute to making you whole.*

☾ Reflection Affirmation ☽

I embrace my emotions fully, knowing they are a source of strength and authenticity in my journey.

☾ 3 Things I Learned ☽

1.

2.

3.

★ *Key Insights and Takeaways:*

"In the midst of darkness, light persists."

– Mahatma Gandhi

6

GETTING STARTED WITH SHADOW WORK

GETTING STARTED WITH SHADOW WORK

Shadow work is the process of exploring and embracing the hidden aspects of ourselves. It contributes to profound personal growth and development. These exercises are designed to help you connect with yourself on a deeper level. Appreciate all aspects of who you are while simultaneously bringing attention to unfamiliar parts of yourself. The goal is to take the negative stigma away from traits you deem unacceptable, and also understanding your shadow and what contributes to some of your less desirable behavior.

Just as the sun casts shadows, so too do our inner struggles, but by shining a light on them, we can navigate through the darkness to find greater clarity, authenticity, and ultimately, liberation. As you commence your shadow work, a slow metamorphosis will gently begin, and you will feel like a phoenix rising from its own ashes.

MIRROR WORK: *Intimate Reflections*

Mirror work, also known as mirror gazing, is a technique used in shadow work as a powerful method for self-reflection. By gazing into a mirror and observing yourself without judgment, you can confront your shadow self. This is the part of our psyche that contains repressed emotions, fears, and unresolved issues.

By acknowledging and integrating these aspects, we gain a deeper understanding of ourselves and can move towards wholeness and healing. Windows are the eyes to the soul, so when you begin to engage in mirror work, it opens a direct path to the heart of our shadow, wherein lies our discomfort and distress.

Mirrors have the power to evoke strong emotions, serving as helpful tools for shifting our perspective and revealing hidden aspects of ourselves that we might otherwise overlook while focusing outwardly.

Practicing mirror work regularly will help you explore emotional symptoms and pinpoint underlying causes easier. Often, people shy away from confronting their mistakes or acknowledging aspects of themselves they perceive as flawed. However, in front of a mirror, there's no escaping our errors and imperfections, and we can confront ourselves at any time.

Although looking at oneself in a mirror can be uncomfortable, particularly when it highlights imperfections and weaknesses, this technique develops greater self-compassion. By confronting our reflections, we can gradually acknowledge our flaws and embrace a more realistic, forgiving perspective. Once you understand imperfection is universal and doesn't diminish our worthiness of love — especially when it comes to loving ourselves.

Our innate desire to be seen and reflected is fundamental to our understanding of ourselves. As children, we learn about ourselves through the reflections provided by those around us. Psychology studies have shown the importance of face-to-face interaction for our social and emotional development. In an increasingly digital world, where solitude and screens dominate, we risk missing out on this crucial social contact.

✶ *Mirror Work Exercise:*

Find a comfortable spot and draw close to the mirror, focusing your eyes to meet your reflection head-on. Allow your mind to become still, letting go of any thoughts or distractions.

Take a moment to observe what aspects of yourself you may struggle with, whether it's a physical imperfection or an internal struggle. Once you've pinpointed it, begin to shower yourself with positive affirmations.

Keep your gaze fixed on your reflection, engaging in a dialogue with yourself rather than shutting your eyes. This practice delves into intimacy as you spend mindful moments with your own reflection, confronting not just your thoughts but also your own scrutinizing eyes. You might even view the mirror as your personal adversary, reflecting mixed feelings you hold toward yourself.

Be open to whatever experiences or insights may arise. If your mind starts to wander or thoughts arise, gently bring your focus back to the reflection. Continue to maintain a state of mindfulness and receptivity. Trust in the process and be patient with yourself.

Dedicate 5-10 minutes to maintaining eye contact with yourself, resisting the urge to look away. If you're at ease, engage in conversation with your reflection, perhaps even conversing with your shadow. When you're ready to conclude, reassure yourself that you are safe and cherished.

Through this exercise, extend compassion and affection to yourself. Embrace the opportunity to grapple with your inner struggles and embrace your vulnerabilities with kindness and acceptance.

1. Find a quiet and comfortable space where you won't be disturbed.
2. Set up a mirror in front of you at eye level.
3. Sit in a relaxed position in front of the mirror.
4. Take a few deep breaths to center yourself and relax.
5. Gaze into your own eyes in the mirror. Maintain a soft focus.
6. Allow yourself to be present with whatever thoughts and emotions arise.
7. You can use affirmations or ask yourself questions to facilitate self-reflection.
8. Be patient and open to whatever insights or feelings may come up.
9. After some time, gently end the session and take note of any reflections or insights you gained.

Remember, mirror work is a personal practice, so feel free to adjust these steps to suit your own preferences and needs.

Some positive affirmations you can say to yourself in the mirror are:

- I love and approve of myself.
- I am grateful for my life.
- I am worthy of love and happiness.
- I am beautiful just the way I am.

Create your own positive affirmations in the chat bubbles below that you can use for your mirror work gazing sessions.

Mirror Work Reflections

☾ As you gazed into the mirror, what aspects of yourself did you struggle to accept, and how can you cultivate greater self-love and compassion in those areas?

☾ Reflect on a recent challenge or setback you've faced. How does your reflection in the mirror embody resilience, and what affirmations can you repeat to reinforce your strength?

☾ Imagine your reflection in the mirror as a wise mentor. What advice would your reflection offer you about pursuing your dreams and embracing your true potential?

☾ As you gaze into the mirror, what emotions arise? Reflect on the feelings that surface and explore their origins.

☾ Imagine the person staring back at you is your closest friend. What advice or encouragement would you offer them based on what you see?

☾ What aspects of yourself do you often overlook or ignore? Take a few moments to acknowledge and appreciate those parts of yourself as you look in the mirror.

IDENTIFYING PATTERNS

Shadow work involves delving into the parts of ourselves that we often keep hidden or suppressed. Identifying patterns within this work is crucial for understanding recurring themes or behaviors that may be holding us back from growth and self-actualization. By recognizing these patterns, we can begin to address them and work towards healing and integration.

Examples of Patterns in Shadow Work and What to Do About Them:

★ *Self-Sabotage:*
Recognizing behaviors or thoughts that undermine our own success or well-being. To address this, practice self-compassion and explore underlying beliefs driving the sabotage.

★ *People-Pleasing:*
Consistently prioritizing others' needs over our own, often at the expense of our own happiness. Set boundaries and practice assertiveness to honor your own needs.

★ *Avoidance:*
Avoiding difficult emotions or situations instead of confronting them. Practice mindfulness and cultivate a willingness to sit with discomfort to facilitate growth.

★ *Perfectionism:*
Setting impossibly high standards and feeling inadequate when unable to meet them Practice self-acceptance and embrace imperfection as part of the human experience.

★ *Fear of Failure:*
Paralyzed by the fear of making mistakes or falling short of expectations. Reframe failure as a learning opportunity and celebrate efforts rather than just outcomes.

★ *Attachment Patterns:*
Unhealthy attachment styles that affect relationships, such as codependency or avoidant behavior. Seek therapy to explore attachment wounds and develop healthier relationship dynamics.

Identifying these patterns is just the first step. It's important to approach them with curiosity and compassion, understanding that they often stem from past experiences and conditioning. Working through these patterns can lead to greater self-awareness, emotional resilience, and personal growth.

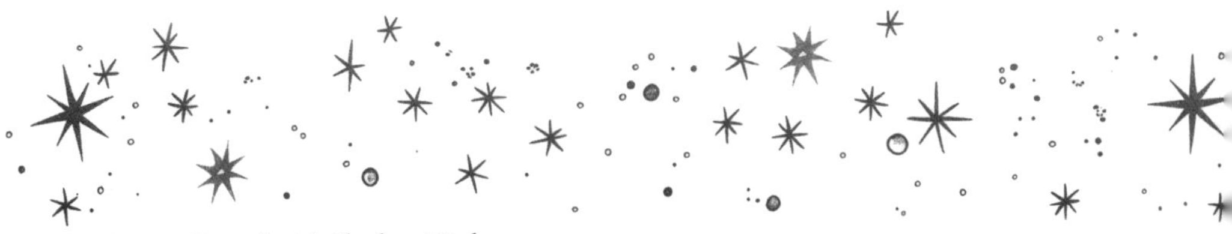

☾ What do you struggle with most in your life?

☾ What patterns do you see repeating themselves in your life?

☾ How does it make you feel when a pattern shows up in your life that is unhealthy?

☾ What patterns are you mimicking from your parents?

☾ What can you change or do differently to break those patterns?

IDENTIFYING ADULT TRAUMA & TRIGGERS

Understanding adult traumas and triggers is crucial for shadow work, as they often unearth unhealed wounds from our past. Traumas can range from childhood experiences to recent events, shaping our reactions and behaviors in adulthood. Triggers, on the other hand, are stimuli that evoke emotional responses tied to these traumas. Exploring these traumas and triggers through shadow work involves delving into the depths of our subconscious to bring awareness to these unresolved issues, allowing for healing and personal growth.

Below is a list of potential traumas you may have experienced in adolescence or adulthood. Identifying them is crucial for initiating the healing process. Trauma and triggers are closely linked. Recognizing the triggers associated with trauma is key to understanding your behaviors and reactions. This awareness can alleviate the guilt you may feel during adverse reactions. By comprehending the underlying trauma and its triggers, you can start developing a plan to address it and heal from them.

This is only a select list of traumas. Circle all the traumas you have experienced. There is room to add additional traumas that may not be listed.

DEATH OF A PARENT

DEATH OF A SIBLING

DEATH OF A GRANDPARENT

DEATH OF A FAMILY MEMBER

DEATH OF A PET

DEATH OF A FRIEND

ABANDONMENT BY PARENT

ABANDONMENT BY PARTNER

NEGLECT BY PARENT

NEGLECT BY PARTNER

PHYSICAL ABUSE BY PARENT

PHYSICAL ABUSE BY PARTNER

MENTAL OR EMOTIONAL ABUSE

CAR ACCIDENT

____

____

____

____

LIFE-THREATENING INJURIES

MINOR INJURIES

NEAR-DEATH EXPERIENCE

BETRAYAL BY PARTNER

LOSING A JOB

FINANCIAL STRUGGLES

HOMELESSNESS

DRUG USE

ALCOHOL USE

POOR SELF ESTEEM

WORK-RELATED ISSUES

CANCER/DISEASE

MENTAL ILLNESS

WITNESSING A TRAUMATIC EVENT

____

____

____

____

Below are some common triggers that can act as a catalyst for manifesting negative behaviors that stem from past traumas. Circle any trigger that is applicable to you. There's space below to add any additional triggers that are specific to you

TRAFFIC CONGESTION

LOUD NOISES

YELLING OR RAISED VOICES

BEING INTERRUPTED

FEELING IGNORED OR DISMISSED

FEELING CONTROLLED OR MANIPULATED

FEELING JUDGED OR CRITICIZED

FEELING ABANDONED OR REJECTED

EXPERIENCING FAILURE OR SETBACKS

WITNESSING INJUSTICE OR UNFAIRNESS

FEELING INADEQUATE OR NOT GOOD ENOUGH

EXPERIENCING LOSS OR SEPARATION

FEELING OVERWHELMED OR OUT OF CONTROL

FACING CONFRONTATION OR CONFLICT

FEELING VULNERABLE OR EXPOSED

BEING JUDGED

BEING REJECTED

Use the trigger tree below to work through your main trigger so you can pave a road to healing.

Healing after identifying triggers and traumas in shadow work involves a journey of self-compassion and acceptance. It requires acknowledging the pain and vulnerability that arise from confronting these aspects of oneself. By embracing these shadows with empathy and understanding, one can begin to integrate them into their whole self, fostering inner harmony and growth. Healing may involve various practices such as therapy, mindfulness, and self-care rituals tailored to individual needs. Through this process, individuals can cultivate resilience, reclaim their power, and ultimately experience greater wholeness and authenticity in their lives.

Now that you've identified some traumas and triggers it's time to pave the way for healing.

☾ What events from the past hurt me?

☾ What do I want to heal from?

☾ What things have I healed from already? How did I heal from them?

☾ Who has helped me heal in the past? Can I ask them for help again?

☾ Where do I feel most at peace? Where can I go to heal?

☾ Reflect on a past trauma that still haunts you. Describe how it has shaped your beliefs and behaviors.

☾ Imagine yourself encountering a trigger related to your trauma. How do you react? What thoughts and emotions arise?

☾ Explore the origins of your triggers. What past experiences contributed to their development?

☾ Visualize a safe space where you can confront your triggers without fear. Describe this space in detail and how it makes you feel.

☾ Describe a recent experience where you felt triggered. How did you manage the situation, and what did you learn from it?

☾ Imagine yourself as a compassionate observer, witnessing your own healing journey. What do you notice about your progress and setbacks?

DIALOGUE WITH THE SHADOW

Create a quiet space where you can sit with your thoughts without distraction. Begin by imagining your shadow as a separate presence—maybe it has a shape, a voice, or an energy that feels familiar. Open a written dialogue with it, using a two-column or script-style format. Write your question or statement on one side (as you), and let the shadow respond freely (as it).

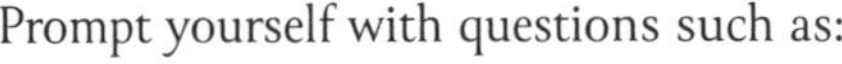

Prompt yourself with questions such as:

- What do you want me to understand about myself?
- What are you trying to protect me from?
- What part of my past do you carry most heavily?
- What would happen if I stopped ignoring you?

Let the tone of the shadow be honest—even if it feels critical, defensive, or emotional. Your goal is to listen, not to fix.

You:	*Your Shadow:*

SYMBOLIC RELEASE RITUAL

Transform inner release into a physical act. This ritual helps externalize what you're letting go of—whether it's a belief, emotion, memory, or identity tied to your shadow—through symbolic action.

✶ *Write It Down*

On a small piece of paper, write down what you're ready to release. It could be a limiting belief "I am not enough," a memory that still holds pain, a behavior you've outgrown, or an identity that no longer fits.

✶ *Create a Release Vessel*

Choose a symbolic action that resonates with you:

- ☾ Tear it up and bury it in the earth
- ☾ Fold it into a leaf or flower and release it into a stream or natural space
- ☾ Seal it in an envelope and store it as a ritual marker of your growth

✶ *Seal the Practice*

Once you've released the paper, place your hand over your heart and take a few slow breaths. Say aloud or silently:

"I let go of what no longer serves me. I reclaim my energy."

"We delight in the beauty of the butterfly, but rarely admit the changes it has gone through to achieve that beauty."

THE METAMORPHOSIS WITHIN

Before a butterfly takes flight, it undergoes one of the most profound transformations in nature. It begins as a caterpillar—earthbound and instinct-driven, focused on survival and consumption. Then, it surrenders to stillness within the chrysalis, where everything it once was breaks down. This isn't just a phase—it's a full dissolution of form, a surrender into the unknown.

Inside that cocoon, the caterpillar becomes unrecognizable. Cells that once served its crawling life dissolve. It's dark. Isolating. Uncertain. But within that darkness, new structures begin to form—delicate wings, antennae, beauty that did not exist before. Only through this deep and hidden process does the butterfly emerge. Transformed. Whole. Free.

We often admire the end result—the grace, the colors, the ability to fly—but forget what it took to get there. Just like the butterfly, personal transformation requires us to pass through stages of discomfort, unlearning, and unseen internal work. Shadow growth is the chrysalis. The dark place. The deconstruction. But it is not the end. It is the becoming.

From Cocoon to Flight

✶ *Acknowledging the Cocoon*

Reflect on your own chrysalis phase—times when you felt isolated, confused, or like everything was falling apart.

- ☾ What part of your identity felt like it was dissolving during that time?
- ☾ What emotions or beliefs were most present in that "in-between" space?
- ☾ How did the world around you misunderstand your stillness or struggle?

✶ *Identifying the Wings*

Now think about what quietly began forming within you, even if no one else could see it.

- ☾ What strengths, insights, or new perspectives emerged from that darkness?
- ☾ What parts of you were being built in silence?
- ☾ What can you now recognize as beautiful, that only came from your past pain?

✶ *Task: Create Your Metamorphosis Symbol*

Draw, collage, or describe a symbol that represents your shadow-to-light journey so far. It doesn't have to be a butterfly—choose any image or form that captures your transformation (a cracked seed, a rising moon, shifting tides). Label the parts that show the before, the in-between, and the emerging you.

✶ *Grounding Action: Affirmation Ritual*

Write a personal affirmation inspired by your journey. Stand in front of a mirror and say it aloud:

Repeat this daily during a transitional or emotionally heavy period. Add your own ending if desired—something specific and true to your story.

EMOTION ARMOR INVENTORY

Throughout life, we unconsciously develop emotional armor—protective behaviors, expressions, or even personalities we wear to keep ourselves safe from feeling certain emotions. This armor isn't just avoidance—it's adaptation. Shadow work involves identifying where we've armored up, why, and how it's kept us both protected and disconnected.

Instructions:

1. Choose One Emotion You Rarely Show.
(Examples: Vulnerability, grief, jealousy, helplessness, tenderness, rage)

2. Reflect: What armor do I wear instead?

Use these prompts:

☾ What do I do to cover this emotion up? (e.g., humor, control, silence, people-pleasing)

☾ How do I want to be seen instead of what I feel?

☾ Where did I learn to hide this emotion—home, school, relationships?

3. List Your Emotional Armor Pieces

Give them names or roles. For example:

- ☾ **"The Achiever"** to cover up fear of failure
- ☾ **"The Tough One"** to protect sadness
- ☾ **"The Peacemaker"** to avoid anger
- ☾ **"The Entertainer"** to mask loneliness
- ☾ Create a Personal **"Armor Profile"**

Draw a figure or outline below and label it with the armor you wear in different emotional states. Note the cost: What does this protect me from—and what does it keep me from experiencing fully?

✶ *Integration Task:*

Choose one piece of emotional armor. For a day or a moment, set it down. Practice naming the real emotion underneath it when it arises—even if just to yourself. Observe how it feels to be exposed without it.

DREAM ANALYSIS

Carl Jung viewed dream analysis as a fundamental tool for understanding the unconscious mind and exploring the depths of the psyche. He believed that dreams offered valuable insights into one's psyche, serving as a bridge between the conscious and unconscious realms. Jung emphasized the symbolic nature of dreams, suggesting that each dream symbol represents a potential aspect of the dreamer's inner world. Through careful interpretation and exploration of dream symbols, individuals could gain profound self-awareness and uncover hidden aspects of their personality. Overall, Jung considered dream analysis to be a vital component of psychotherapy and personal growth.

At times, our dreams prompt us to embrace aspects of our psyche or ourselves that we've neglected, turning dream analysis into a journey through our shadows. Alternatively, our dreams might lead us into the essence of our existence, where distinctions blur and conditioning fades away.

☾ Reflect on the recurring symbols or motifs in your dreams. What do you think they represent in your subconscious?

☾ Describe the emotions you felt during your dream. How did they differ from your waking emotions?

☾ Consider the interactions you had with dream characters. How do they reflect your relationships or inner thoughts?

☾ Think about the lessons or messages you believe your dreams are trying to convey to you. How can you apply them to your daily life?

Dreamwork during shadow work involves paying close attention to the content of your dreams, as they often contain insights into your subconscious desires, fears, and unresolved issues. Here's how you can integrate dreamwork into your shadow work:

✶ *Dream Journaling:*
Keep a dream journal by your bed and write down your dreams as soon as you wake up. Record as much detail as possible, including emotions, symbols, and any significant events or people.

✶ *Symbol Interpretation:*
Analyze the symbols and themes in your dreams.
Look for recurring patterns or symbols that may represent aspects of your shadow self.

✶ *Reflective Practice:*
Take time to reflect on the meaning of your dreams.
Consider how they relate to your waking life, your emotions, and any unresolved conflicts or traumas.

✶ *Active Imagination:*
Engage in active imagination techniques to explore the deeper meaning of your dreams. This involves entering into a dialogue with the characters or symbols in your dreams to gain insight into your subconscious.

✶ *Integration:*
Use the insights gained from your dreamwork to inform your shadow work practice. Look for connections between your dreams, your conscious thoughts, and behaviors, then use this information to identify and work through any unresolved issues or patterns.

By incorporating dreamwork into your shadow work practice, you can gain a deeper understanding of your subconscious mind and accelerate your personal growth and healing process.

Dream Journal

Today's Date: ____/____/____ S M T W T F S

✶ What happened?

✶ How I feel:

	Yes	No
✶ Interrupted?	☐	☐
✶ Recurring?	☐	☐

✶ Vivid Imagery: (draw below)

✶ My Interpretation:

✶ Sleep Quality:

low ⟵⟶ high

○ ○ ○ ○ ○ ○ ○ ○ ○

✶ Notes:

Dream Journal

Today's Date: ____/____/____ S M T W T F S

✶ *What happened?*

✶ *How I feel:*

	Yes	*No*
✶ *Interrupted?*	☐	☐
✶ *Recurring?*	☐	☐

✶ *Vivid Imagery:* (draw below)

✶ *My Interpretation:*

✶ *Sleep Quality:*

low ← → *high*

○ ○ ○ ○ ○ ○ ○ ○ ○

✶ *Notes:*

Dream Journal

Today's Date: ____/____/____ S M T W T F S

✶ *What happened?*

✶ *How I feel:*

	Yes	*No*
✶ *Interrupted?*	☐	☐
✶ *Recurring?*	☐	☐

✶ *Vivid Imagery:* (draw below)

✶ *My Interpretation:*

✶ *Sleep Quality:*

low ⟵⟶ *high*

○ ○ ○ ○ ○ ○ ○ ○ ○

✶ *Notes:*

Dream Journal

Today's Date: ______/______/______ S M T W T F S

✶ *What happened?*

✶ *How I feel:*

	Yes	No
✶ *Interrupted?*	☐	☐
✶ *Recurring?*	☐	☐

✶ *Vivid Imagery:* (draw below)

✶ *My Interpretation:*

✶ *Sleep Quality:*

low ⟵⟶ *high*

○ ○ ○ ○ ○ ○ ○ ○ ○

✶ *Notes:*

GRATITUDE PRACTICES:
Simple Steps to Feel More Thankful and Happy

Gratitude is like a gentle light that brightens even the shadowy parts of our lives. It's about recognizing and appreciating the good, both in the world around us and within ourselves. This exercise is dedicated to cultivating a spirit of thankfulness, which can transform your perspective and bring a deeper sense of joy and contentment.

✶ *Gratitude Mapping: Day 1*

Take 10 minutes to write down what you're grateful for in every area of your life. Continue doing this for the next 7 days.

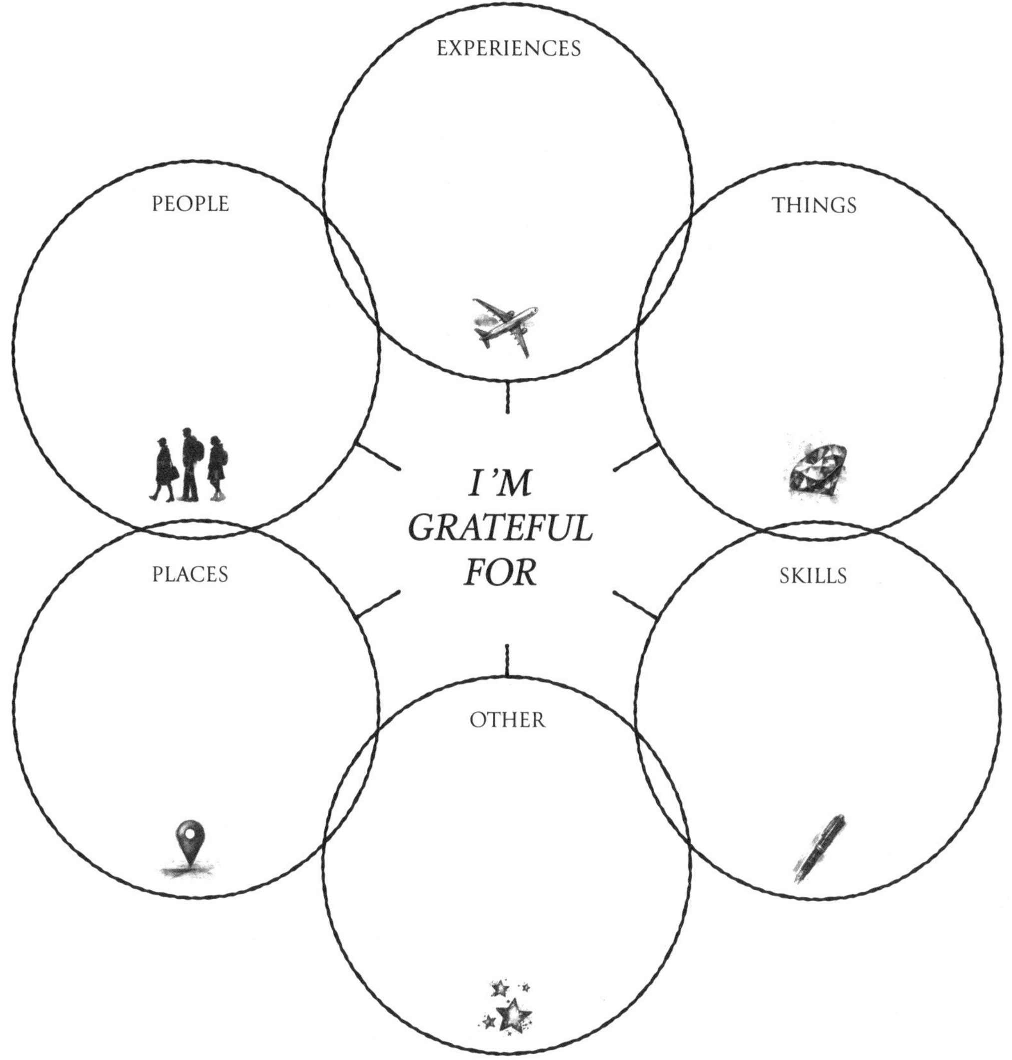

★ *Gratitude Mapping: Day 2*

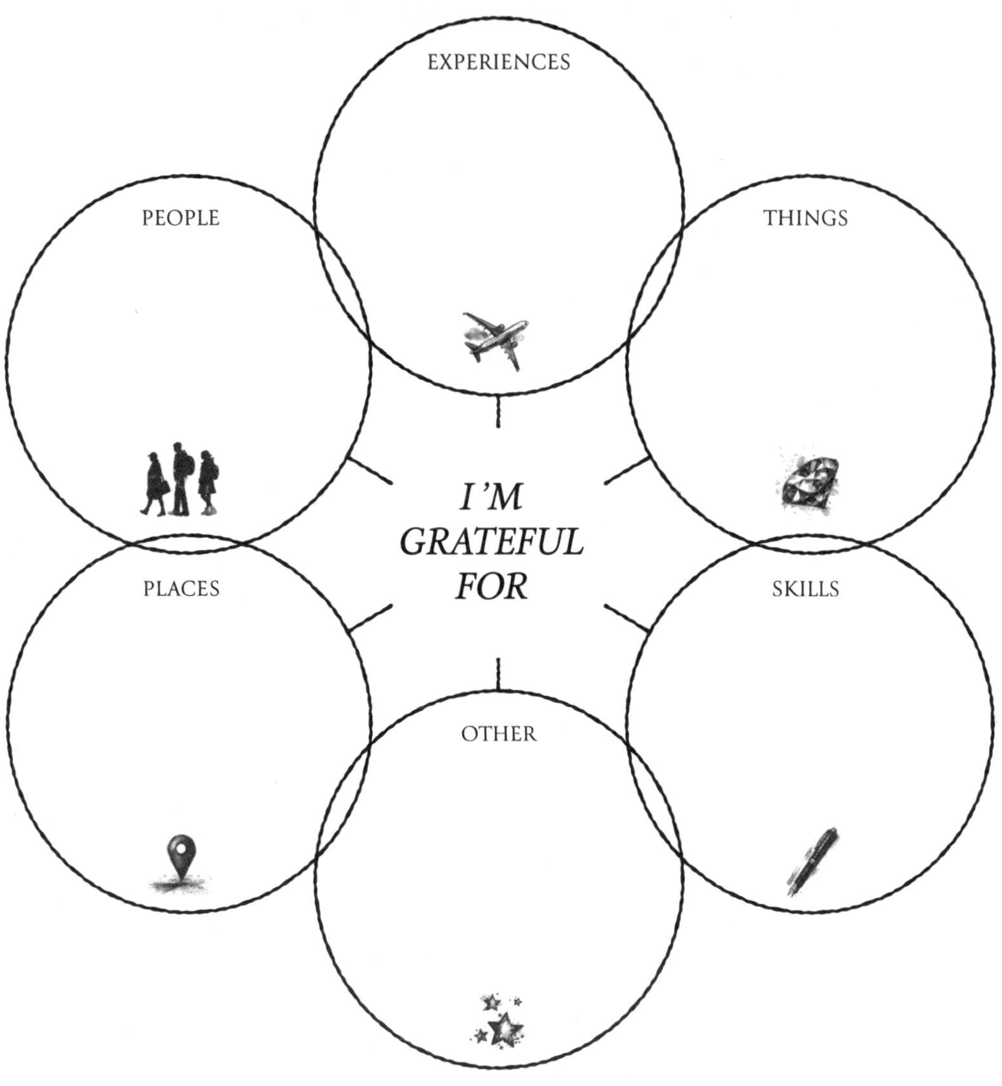

Additional gratitude musings:

✶ *Gratitude Mapping: Day 3*

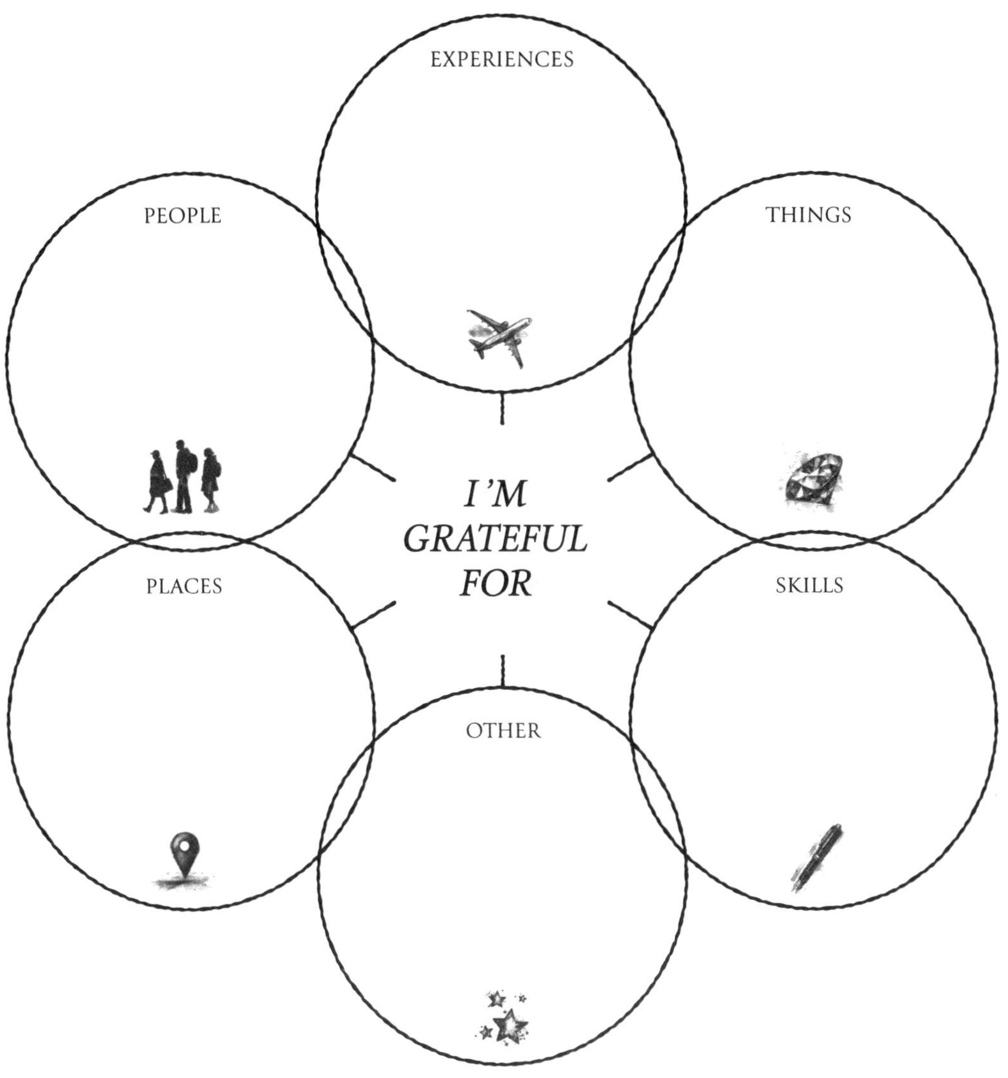

Additional gratitude musings:

★ *Gratitude Mapping: Day 4*

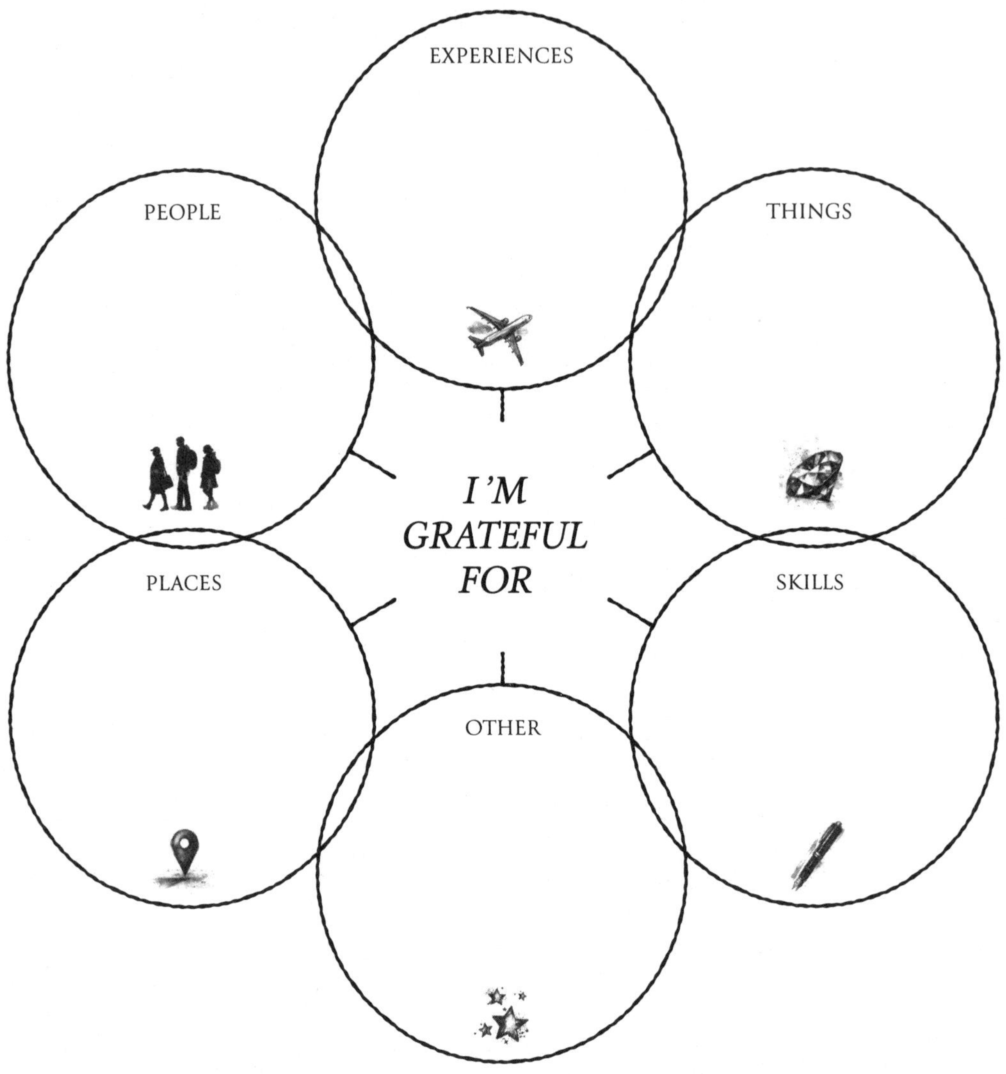

Additional gratitude musings:

✶ *Gratitude Mapping: Day 5*

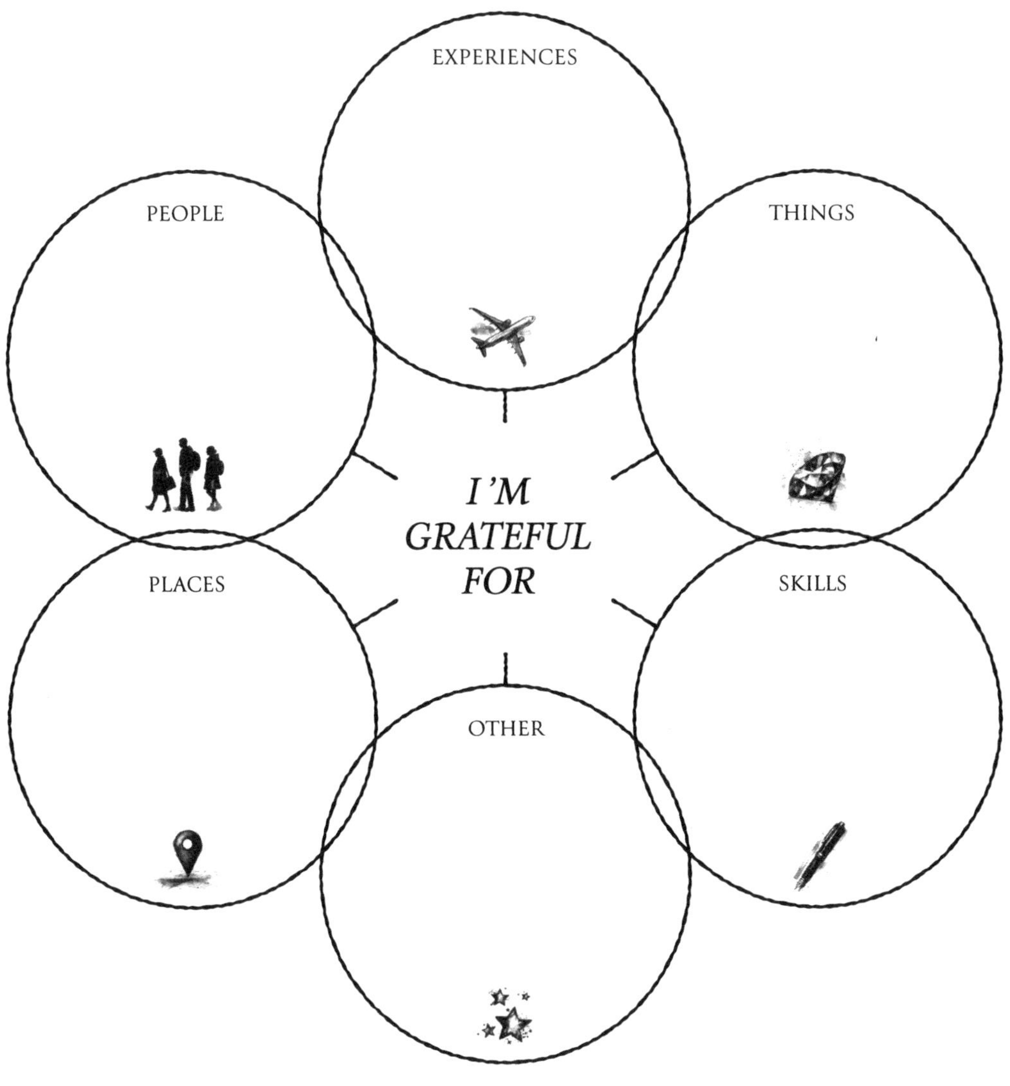

Additional gratitude musings:

✶ *Gratitude Mapping: Day 6*

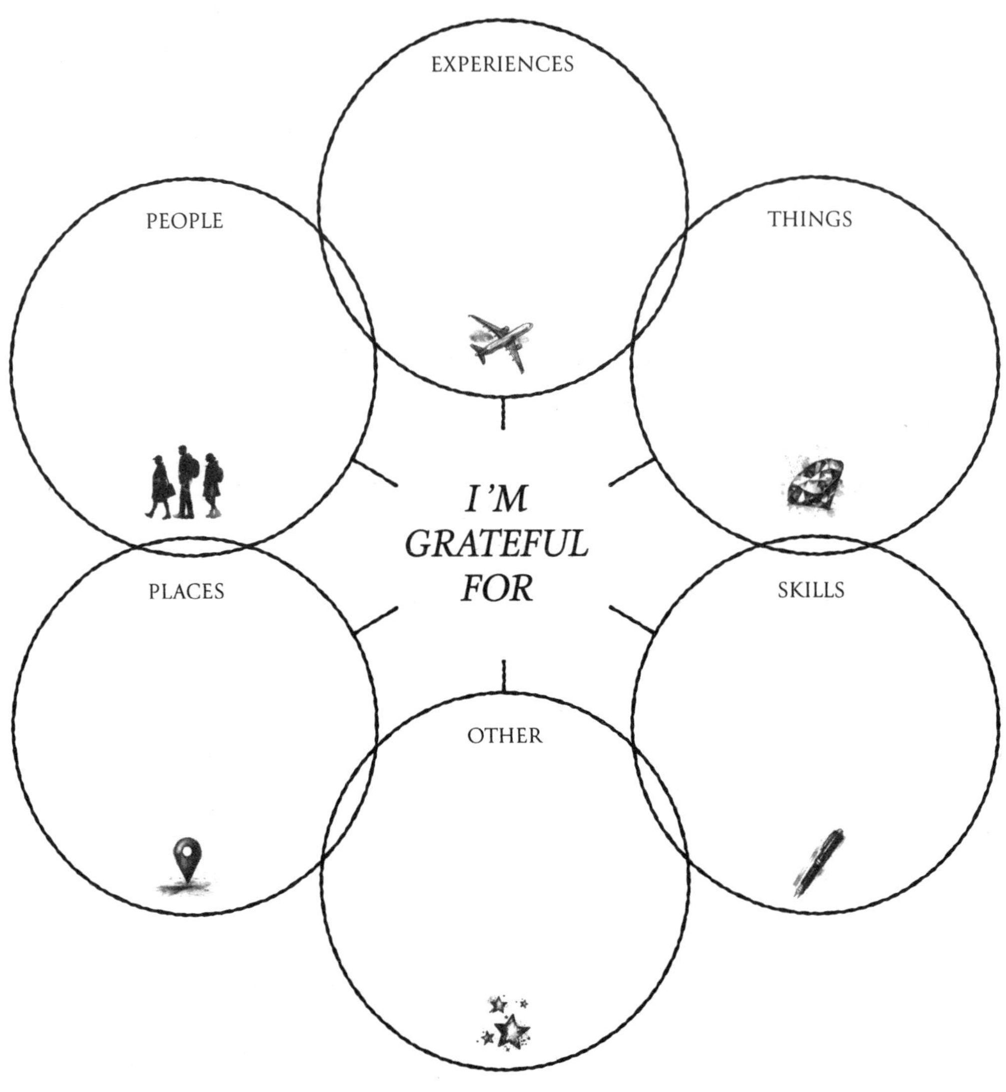

Additional gratitude musings:

✶ *Gratitude Mapping: Day 7*

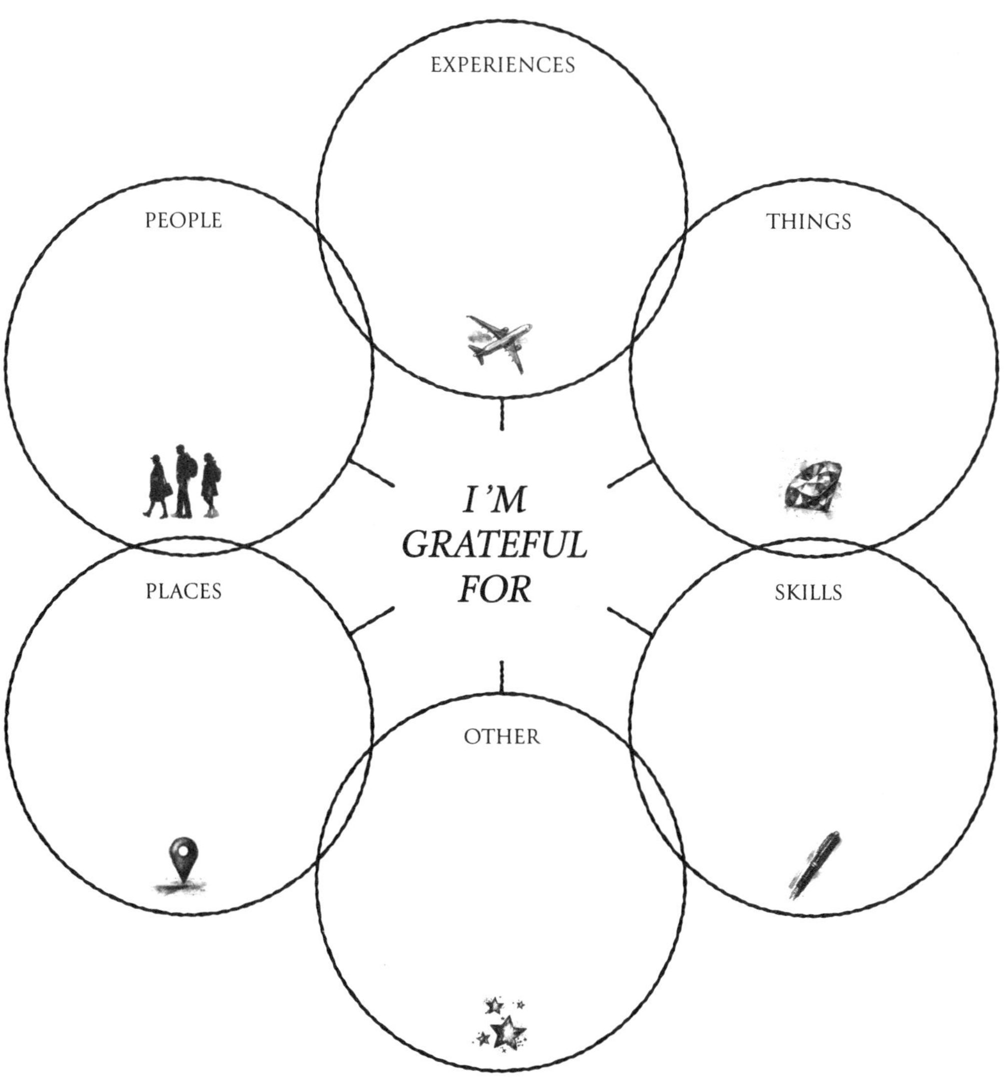

Additional gratitude musings:

☾ Reflect on someone who has positively impacted your life and write a letter expressing gratitude to them.

Dear ______________________,

Sincerely,

☾ Go outside and take a moment to appreciate the beauty in nature around you. Describe a specific scene or moment that brings you joy.

☾ Consider a challenging situation you've overcome recently and write about what you learned from it.

☾ Think about three things you appreciate about yourself and why.

☾ Recall a recent act of kindness you received from someone and express your gratitude for their gesture.

☾ Think about a small pleasure you often overlook, like a favorite food or a comforting routine, and write about why it brings you happiness.

☾ Reflect on a moment from today that brought you joy, no matter how small, and express gratitude for experiencing it.

☾ Write about a supportive friend or family member and how they've helped you during difficult times.

☾ Reflect on a privilege or opportunity you have in your life and write about how it has benefited you.

☾ Consider a skill or talent you possess and reflect on how it has enriched your life or the lives of others.

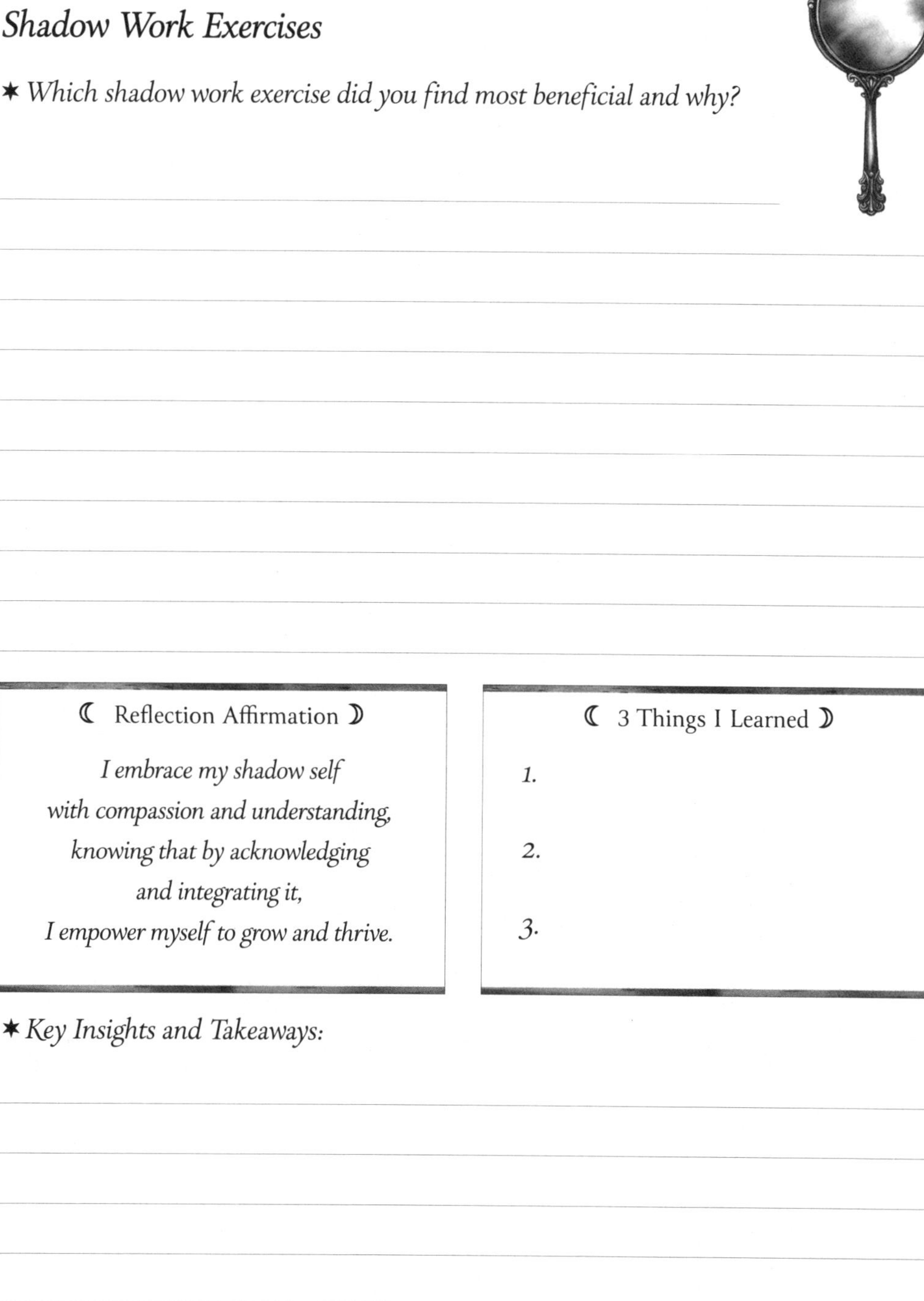

REFLECTION POINT: Shadow Work Exercises

★ *Which shadow work exercise did you find most beneficial and why?*

☾ Reflection Affirmation ☽

I embrace my shadow self
with compassion and understanding,
knowing that by acknowledging
and integrating it,
I empower myself to grow and thrive.

☾ 3 Things I Learned ☽

1.

2.

3.

★ *Key Insights and Takeaways:*

"There is strong shadow where there is much light."

– Johann Wolfgang von Goethe

7

SELF-CARE PRACTICES TO PARTNER WITH SHADOW WORK

TECHNIQUES FOR TRANQUILITY & RELAXATION

Remember, shadow work can be challenging. It can bring up repressed memories or feelings that can be difficult to deal with. You will be exploring uncomfortable territory and self-care, and wellness should be incorporated into your journey. It's imperative you take it one step at a time and combine relaxing techniques into your shadow work routine.

This section of your journal serves as a sanctuary for moments of peace and reflection. Within these pages, you'll discover simple, mindful exercises and techniques crafted to guide you towards tranquility and insight during your shadow work journey. These practices are designed to foster a calm and deeper understanding as you explore your experiences, thoughts, and emotions.

Calming Your Mind and Heart: Basic Mindfulness and Meditation for Beginners

In the following pages, you will find basic meditation scripts for various types of meditation. It's recommended that you pre-record the script you select and play it back while you meditate so you can completely submerse yourself in the peacefulness of the experience.

Grounding Meditation Techniques

Grounding meditation is a practice that fosters connection with the earth, aiming to center oneself and enhance feelings of vitality and alertness. Our bodies possess electrical conductivity, and earth acts as a large battery to balance out and recharge our bodies, thus working as an extremely powerful antioxidant. In today's world, the abundance of rubber-soled shoes insulates us from the earth's free electrons, hindering this natural exchange. Grounding, also known as Earthing, involves walking barefoot on natural surfaces like sand, dirt, or grass, allowing our bodies to absorb beneficial ions from the earth's surface, acting as antioxidants.

Next, we've outlined several guided grounding meditation techniques for you to explore and find what resonates best with you. To receive the most benefits from grounding, stay connected to the earth for a minimum of 20 minutes. This allows for a sufficient electron transfer.

✶ *Grounding (Earthing)*

To practice grounding, make direct contact with the earth using your body, such as your feet, legs, or hands, creating an electrical connection to the ground. This contact with the earth can produce healing effects down to the cellular level. Decide whether you want to stand barefoot, sit with your legs extended touching the ground, or lay down with your whole body touching the ground.

Once you're ready to begin, close your eyes and visualize roots extending from the bottoms of your feet deep into the ground. Feel the vitality of the Earth ascending through these roots into your being. Envision yourself being enveloped in the earth's energy, feeling the vibrations and power surging within you. With every inhalation, allow this light to imbue you with serenity and peace, dispelling any negativity or restlessness.

Continue breathing deeply, and with each breath, affirm to yourself: "I am anchored, I am secure, I am serene."

Remain in this relaxed state for however long feels right. When you're ready, gradually return your focus to the present moment.

Write about your grounding (earthing) meditation experience below:

★ *Grounding Moon Meditation*

This practice can be performed indoors if the moon is visible, yet it's optimal to do it outside in the fresh air. Let all the worries and thoughts accumulated during the day drift away on the night breeze. Imagine each troubling thought forming a ball and rolling away from you effortlessly.

Stand or sit in your chosen spot and surrender yourself to the moon's glow. Take deep breaths, exhaling slowly. Observe the moon in your sky, noting any subtle differences from your expectations. Embrace these differences as a part of your present reality. Acknowledge that the only moment you truly exist in is now, with this moon in your sky. Whatever you wished for is in the past, and whatever may come is in the future.

Tomorrow's moon will be different, just as yesterdays was. Focus on the present moment. With your eyes closed, find stillness within yourself. Straighten your back and feel every worry, anger, or fear dissipate as you embrace peace. When your mind has settled and silence surrounds you, repeat the following to yourself: ***"I am alive. I am present. I am safe."***

Write about your grounding moon meditation experience below:

✶ *Grounding Sun Meditation*

This practice is best done outdoors, preferably on a sunny day. Choose whether to sit or stand based on your comfort. You can also decide whether to keep your eyes open or closed for better focus. Find a spot with ample sunlight, leaving shadows behind as you step into the light.

Begin by gently pushing away any other worries, tasks, or thoughts, and focus your awareness on the warmth of the sun on your skin. Visualize the sunlight as a comforting hug, dispelling doubts and easing fears. Direct your attention specifically to how the sunlight feels on your chest.

Take a moment to fully explore this sensation. As you bask in the sun, envision the warmth in your chest expanding, fueled by the glorious sunlight. Feel it spreading through your entire body, filling every pore, strengthening and empowering you. Imagine the sun sharing its power, imparting its radiance and glow upon you. This newfound energy allows you to stand taller and shine brighter.

Once the warmth has permeated every inch of your being, carry this feeling with you throughout your day, knowing that the sun's guidance is always with you. Repeat in your mind: ***"I am radiant, I am glowing, and I am powerful."***

Write about your grounding sun meditation experience below:

BODY SCAN MEDITATION

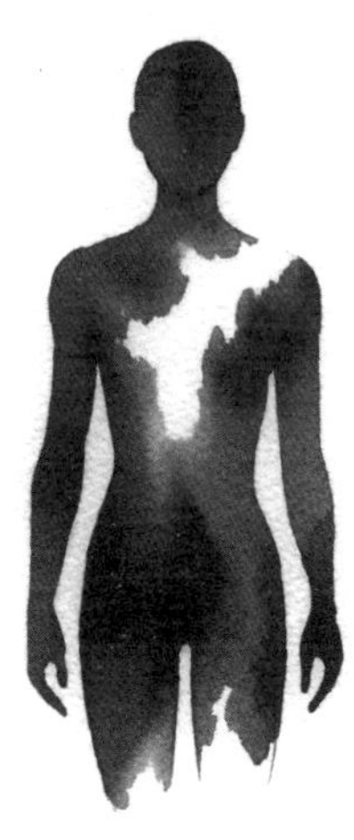

Body Scan Meditation Involves systematically focusing on different parts of the body, often starting from the toes and moving up to the head, to increase awareness of bodily sensations and promote relaxation. The body scan is a mindfulness meditation practice that involves systematically scanning your body for any sensations, such as pain, tension, or anything else out of the ordinary. It can be a helpful tool for fostering a deeper connection to both your physical and emotional self.

For the next several minutes, dedicate your focus to the physical sensations coursing through your body. These sensations may include the touch of fabric against your skin, the subtle tension nestled within your muscles, the ambient temperature enveloping you, or any other tactile experience available to you. At times, you may find yourself not sensing anything at all.

Begin by directing the attention of your mind inward, towards your own body. Endeavor to filter out external noises, disturbances, and even intrusive thoughts. Locate a serene, comfortable environment to commence this practice. Close your eyes; the act of sight often triggers your brain to interpret stimuli. By closing your eyes, you can effectively minimize distractions and delve deeper into your bodily sensations.

Get into a comfortable position, sitting or lying down, ensuring you can fully relax. Remove your shoes and gently close your eyes. Take a deep breath, allowing your body to settle into a state of relaxation.

Begin by focusing your attention on the top of your head. Notice any sensations in this area and gently release any tension you may feel in your scalp, forehead, and temples. Slowly shift your attention down to your face, noticing the muscles in your cheeks, jaw, and around your eyes. Let go of any tension as you focus on the sensations in these areas.

Now, bring your awareness to your neck and shoulders. Notice any tightness or stiffness, and with each breath, imagine the tension dissolving, leaving your neck and shoulders feeling light and relaxed.

Direct your attention to your arms and hands, feeling the weight of your arms and any sensations in your hands. Take a moment to appreciate the feelings in this area. Shift your focus to your chest and abdomen, feeling the gentle rise and fall of your breath.

Allow your breath to deepen naturally, bringing calmness and relaxation to your entire body. Continue moving down your body, noticing any sensations in your hips and backside, without feeling the need to change anything. Focus on your back and spine, feeling the support beneath you and releasing any tension held in your back. Move your awareness to your hips and pelvis, noticing the sensations in this area.

Feel the gentle rhythm of your breath flowing through your body. Finally, bring your attention to your legs and feet, feeling their weight and noticing sensations throughout your feet, including the soles, heel, toes, and top of the foot. As you breathe in, curl your toes, and as you exhale, release your toes along with your breath.

Conclude the body scan exercise at your own pace, and when you're ready, gently open your eyes. Afterwards, fill out the Body Anxiety exercise below to get more in tune with your body.

ON THE FIGURE BELOW, CIRCLE WHERE IN YOUR BODY YOU FEEL TENSION OR STRESS RIGHT NOW. DO A FULL BODY SCAN AND IDENTIFY WHERE YOU TEND TO HOLD YOUR TENSION THAT NEEDS RELAXING.

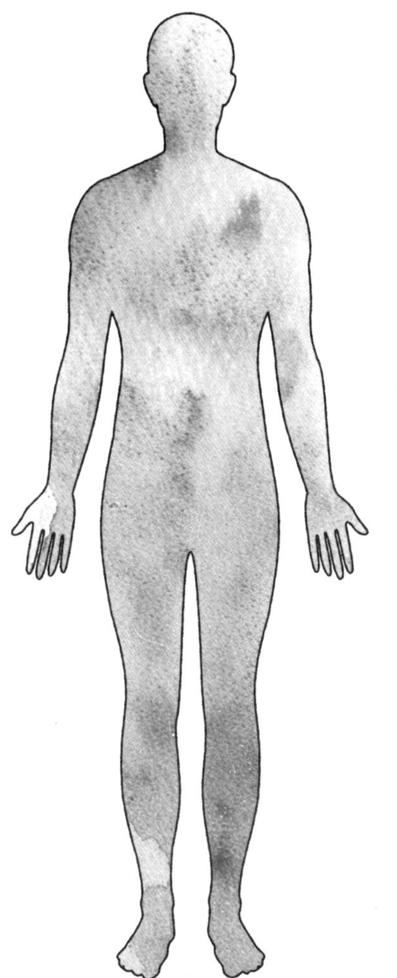

☾ Top 3 Areas of Tension in My Body ☽

1. ______________________

2. ______________________

3. ______________________

After identifying where in your body you feel the most tension, walk through these steps to release it.

1. SIT OR LAY DOWN IN A COMFORTABLE POSITION.
2. START WITH YOUR FACE AND TENSE ALL OF ITS MUSCLES. HOLD FOR THE COUNT OF 8 AS YOU INHALE.
3. EXHALE AND RELAX COMPLETELY. FEEL THE TENSION COMPLETELY RELEASE FROM YOUR FACE.
4. MOVE TO YOUR NECK AND SHOULDERS, AND REPEAT THE SAME PROCESS, TENSING ALL MUSCLES AT THE COUNT OF 8 THEN RELEASING.
5. EXHALE AND RELAX THE NECK AND SHOULDERS COMPLETELY.
6. REPEAT THESE STEPS AS YOU WORK YOUR WAY DOWN THE BODY, CHEST, ARMS, ABDOMEN, BUTT, LEGS AND FEET.

On a scale of 1-10, how does your body feel after this body scan exercise?

1 2 3 4 5 6 7 8 9 10

GRATITUDE MEDITATION

Gratitude meditation is simply the practice of reflecting on the things in our lives we're grateful for. It's about experiencing that feeling of appreciation, whether for a loving family member or friend, a beautiful sunny day, or the pleasure of a good cup of coffee. It's important to note that gratitude isn't just about being thankful for the good things in your life, but for everything in your life. There are aspects of your life that might initially seem unfavorable, but upon further reflection, offer opportunities for learning and growth. Part of gratitude is recognizing blessings in all things, not just the positive. Gratitude will help you appreciate all parts of your shadow. This will help guide you into a place of self-acceptance and love.

Begin by finding a comfortable space that is quiet, quiet is key. Position yourself, either sitting or lying down, allowing your body to relax and your mind to become still. Take a few deep breaths, inhaling slowly through your nose, and exhaling through your mouth. With each breath, feel yourself becoming more grounded and present in this moment. Focus on your breathing and the quiet stillness.

Now, let's bring your attention to the things you're grateful for in your life. They could be big or small, tangible or intangible. With each item, genuinely appreciate it in your heart, feeling the warmth and joy it brings. Keep reflecting on these things, one by one.

As you focus on gratitude, also acknowledge yourself, including your inner shadow. Show yourself compassion and gratitude for all the unique aspects within you. Shift your perspective to see these facets as gifts, noticing how your mood elevates and your perspective broadens. Allow a sense of contentment to wash over you.

Take a few deep breaths, allowing this feeling of gratitude to permeate every cell of your being. When you're ready, gently bring your awareness back to the present moment, carrying this feeling of gratitude with you as you continue your day.

Write about your gratitude meditation experience below:

MEDITATION JOURNAL INTROSPECTIVE: Day 1

Date:	*Length of Time:*
Mantra:	*Meditation style:*
Meditation Focus:	*Location:*

MINDFUL MEDITATION:

Feelings before:	*Feelings after:*

MINDFUL DETAILS:

I am grateful for:

I am working towards:

I am aspiring to do:

MEDITATION JOURNAL INTROSPECTIVE: Day 2

Date: ______________________ *Length of Time:* ______________________

Mantra: ______________________ *Meditation style:* ______________________

Meditation Focus: ______________________ *Location:* ______________________

MINDFUL MEDITATION:

Feelings before:	*Feelings after:*

MINDFUL DETAILS:

I am grateful for: ______________________

I am working towards: ______________________

I am aspiring to do: ______________________

MEDITATION JOURNAL INTROSPECTIVE: Day 3

Date:

Length of Time:

Mantra:

Meditation style:

Meditation Focus:

Location:

MINDFUL MEDITATION:

Feelings before:	*Feelings after:*

MINDFUL DETAILS:

I am grateful for:

I am working towards:

I am aspiring to do:

MEDITATION JOURNAL INTROSPECTIVE: Day 4

Date:

Length of Time:

Mantra:

Meditation style:

Meditation Focus:

Location:

MINDFUL MEDITATION:

Feelings before:	*Feelings after:*

MINDFUL DETAILS:

I am grateful for:

I am working towards:

I am aspiring to do:

MEDITATION JOURNAL INTROSPECTIVE: Day 5

Date:

Length of Time:

Mantra:

Meditation style:

Meditation Focus:

Location:

MINDFUL MEDITATION:

Feelings before:	*Feelings after:*

MINDFUL DETAILS:

I am grateful for:

I am working towards:

I am aspiring to do:

MEDITATION JOURNAL INTROSPECTIVE: Day 6

Date:

Length of Time:

Mantra:

Meditation style:

Meditation Focus:

Location:

MINDFUL MEDITATION:

Feelings before:	*Feelings after:*

MINDFUL DETAILS:

I am grateful for:

I am working towards:

I am aspiring to do:

MEDITATION JOURNAL INTROSPECTIVE: Day 7

Date:

Length of Time:

Mantra:

Meditation style:

Meditation Focus:

Location:

MINDFUL MEDITATION:

Feelings before:	*Feelings after:*

MINDFUL DETAILS:

I am grateful for:

I am working towards:

I am aspiring to do:

REFLECTION POINT: Mindful Meditations

★ *Was this the first time you ever practiced meditation, and would you recommend meditation to others? Why or why not?*

☾ Reflection Affirmation ☽

With each moment of meditation, I cultivate inner peace, clarity, and resilience, embracing the serenity within and around me.

☾ 3 Things I Learned ☽

1.

2.

3.

★ *Key Insights and Takeaways:*

EMOTIONAL FREEDOM TECHNIQUES: A Beginner's Guide to Tapping for Emotional Health

Working with your shadow involves delving into the hidden motivations behind your behavior. With Emotional Freedom Technique (EFT), you directly engage with the subconscious mind, bringing these motivations to the surface through tapping. This gentle technique targets specific acupressure points on the body, addressing traumatic events, emotions, or beliefs. By peeling back each layer of the emotional onion, we uncover the underlying beauty of our true selves. The tapping process aims to restore the natural flow of energy in the body's meridian system, which may have been disrupted by past traumas.

Emotional Freedom Techniques (EFT), often known as tapping, is a method of healing and self-soothing that involves tapping on specific points on the body while focusing on emotions or issues you wish to address. It's a simple yet effective practice for reducing stress, anxiety, and negative emotions. In this section, you'll learn the basics of EFT and how to incorporate it into your shadow work.

★ *Understanding the Tapping Points:*

Before you begin, familiarize yourself with the main tapping points, which are typically:

- ☾ Top of the head
- ☾ Beginning of the eyebrows
- ☾ Side of the eyes
- ☾ Under the eyes
- ☾ Under the nose
- ☾ Chin
- ☾ Beginning of the collarbone
- ☾ Under the arms

You'll gently tap on these points in a sequence while focusing on an emotion or issue.

★ *Choose Your Focus:*

Think about an emotion, memory, or issue you want to work on. It could be something that causes you stress, fear, or discomfort.

★ *The Setup Statement:*

Write a setup statement that acknowledges the issue and affirms self-acceptance. It usually follows this structure: **"Even though I have this [emotion/issue], I deeply and completely accept myself."** Repeat this statement three times while tapping on the side of your hand (the karate chop point).

★ *The Tapping Sequence:*

Now, tap gently on each of the points mentioned earlier, moving down the body. As you tap each point, state a reminder phrase related to your issue, like "this anxiety" or "this fear of failure." Go through the sequence several times while focusing on your feelings.

★ *Reflection & Notes:*

After completing the tapping sequence, take a moment to reflect. Write down any changes you notice in the intensity of your emotion or the clarity of your thoughts. How does your body feel? Do you feel more relaxed, or has your perspective shifted?

★ *Regular Practice:*

Consistency can enhance the effectiveness of EFT. Note in your journal each time you practice tapping and any progress or insights you observe over time. This will help you track your emotional development and the impact of EFT on your well-being.

★ *Closing Thoughts:*

Remember, EFT is a personal and flexible practice. Feel free to adjust the phrases and focus on what resonates with you. It's about finding relief and gaining emotional freedom, so approach it with an open mind and a gentle heart.

EFT can be a powerful tool in your shadow work journey, helping you address and soothe the emotions that emerge. As you continue to use this journal to guide your practice, you'll likely find greater peace and emotional balance.

BREATHING FOR CALM:
Simple Breathing Exercises to Feel Relaxed

Breathing is a powerful tool for calming the mind and soothing the heart. It's something you carry with you everywhere, and with a little focus, it can become a source of great peace and relaxation. In this section, you'll practice simple breathing exercises designed to help you find calm. After each exercise, there's space for you to reflect and write about your experience.

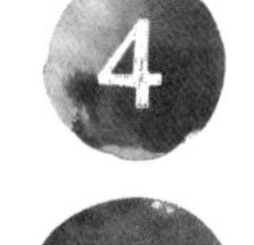

★ *The 4-7-8 Technique:*

This breathing technique is known for its ability to reduce anxiety and promote better sleep. Here's how you do it:

- ☾ Breathe in quietly through your nose for 4 seconds.
- ☾ Hold your breath for 7 seconds.
- ☾ Exhale forcefully through your mouth, pursing your lips and making a *'whoosh'* sound, for 8 seconds.
- ☾ Repeat this cycle four times.

Reflection: After completing the 4-7-8 technique, write about how you felt before and after the exercise. Did your thoughts slow down? How did your body feel? Noting your observations will help you understand how breathing affects your state of mind.

★ *Diaphragmatic Breathing:*

Also known as "belly breathing," this exercise promotes deep, full breaths.

- ☾ Sit comfortably or lie down. Place one hand on your belly and the other on your chest.
- ☾ Breathe in deeply through your nose, feeling your belly rise more than your chest.
- ☾ Exhale slowly through your mouth or nose, feeling your belly fall.
- ☾ Repeat for several minutes.

Reflection: After practicing diaphragmatic breathing, use the space below to write about the experience. **Did you find it easy or challenging to focus on your belly? How did your body and mind respond to the deep breaths?**

★ *Mindful Breathing Observation:*

This exercise encourages you to observe your natural breathing rhythm.

- ☾ Find a quiet place to sit or lie down comfortably.
- ☾ Close your eyes and take a moment to relax your body.
- ☾ Now, simply pay attention to your breath without trying to change it. Notice the sensation of air entering and leaving your nostrils, the rise and fall of your chest or belly, and any other sensations that occur.
- ☾ Continue for a few minutes, gently bringing your attention back to your breath whenever your mind wanders.

Reflection: Write about what you noticed during the mindful breathing observation. Were there any distractions? How did it feel to just observe your breath without altering it?

★ *Regular Practice and Reflection:*

Incorporating these breathing exercises into your daily routine can significantly enhance your ability to find calm and manage stress. As you use your journal to reflect on your experiences, you'll deepen your understanding of how your breath connects to your emotional and physical state.

PROTECT YOUR ENERGY

Engaging in shadow work can indeed be mentally and physically draining initially. It involves confronting uncomfortable or repressed aspects of oneself, which can stir up strong emotions and cause psychological discomfort. This process may lead to feelings of fatigue, emotional exhaustion, and even physical tension as the body responds to the stress of self-exploration.

However, while the process itself may be draining, the long-term effects are often beneficial. As individuals work through their shadow aspects and integrate them into their conscious awareness, they often experience increased mental clarity, emotional stability, and overall well-being, which can ultimately contribute to higher levels of energy in the long run. It's important to balance shadow work with self-care practices to mitigate potential exhaustion and ensure a healthy approach to personal growth.

Since shadow work requires energy and can subsequently drain energy it's important to recognize things that both drain and replenish your energy.

How to deal with ENERGY TAKERS

- ☾ Recognize the people or activities that drain your energy or negatively impact your well being.
- ☾ Establish clear boundaries to protect your time, emotions, and energy from being depleted.
- ☾ Seek out uplifting and supportive individuals who inspire and motivate you.
- ☾ Make self-care a priority by engaging in activities that replenish your energy and bring you joy.
- ☾ Failing to establish clear boundaries with others can lead to feeling overwhelmed.
- ☾ Living or working in a cluttered environment can create mental and physical stress.

ENERGY GIVERS For a better routine

- ☾ Stay organized
- ☾ Get enough sleep
- ☾ Take short breaks
- ☾ Exercise regularly
- ☾ Eat a balanced diet
- ☾ Manage stress
- ☾ Engage in hobbies and passions in order to provide a sense of fulfillment and rejuvenate your energy levels.
- ☾ Spend time with friends and family
- ☾ Spend time outdoors
- ☾ Cultivate a positive mindset and focus on gratitude to improve overall well being
- ☾ Listen to music to uplift your mood

In the section below, write about things (people, scenarios, events) that drain your energy and give you energy. This will help you become mindful of the things to avoid when you feel depleted. In turn, it will also remind you of things you can do to boost and restore your energy.

*"What men call
the shadow
of the body
is not the shadow
of the body,
but is the
body of the soul."*

- Oscar Wilde

8

FINAL REFLECTION

DRAW YOUR SHADOW: PART 2
Comparing Shadows

Earlier in this journal you were asked to draw your shadow. This was before you began your shadow work journey of self-exploration. Thinking about all the exercises you completed and what you learned about yourself, draw your shadow again from this new perspective.

☾ Were there any significant differences between the shadow you drew earlier and the one you drew now? If so, what?

☾ What parts of your shadow are you learning to embrace and how will this impact your daily life?

☾ What shadow trait are you struggling most with and why? What are your plans do integrate it into your life?

AS I GREW OLDER

Langston Hughes 1901 – 1967

It was a long time ago.
I have almost forgotten my dream.
But it was there then,
In front of me, Bright like a sun, -
My dream.
And then the wall rose,
Rose slowly,
Slowly,
Between me and my dream.
Rose slowly, slowly,
Dimming, Hiding,
The light of my dream.
Rose until it touched the sky,—
The wall.
Shadow.
I am black.
I lie down in the shadow.
No longer the light of my dream before me,
Above me.
Only the thick wall.
Only the shadow.
My hands!
My dark hands!
Break through the wall!
Find my dream!
Help me to shatter this darkness,
To smash this night, To break this shadow
Into a thousand lights of sun, Into a thousand
whirling dreams Of sun!

Langston Hughes' "As I Grew Older" is a deeply symbolic and emotional poem that powerfully mirrors the essence of shadow growth, even though it never uses the term directly. The internal struggle is palpable, and the pain leaps from the page with undeniable intensity. Hughes captures the experience of having one's dreams dimmed by unseen forces—something that resonates with anyone who has faced the slow, quiet weight of suppression.

Though the nature of our shadows may differ, the act of confronting them is universal. That shared tension—the desire to reclaim light from darkness—is where shadow work and humanity meet. It is in this collective experience of struggle that we begin to recognize each other, not in perfection, but in the courage it takes to face what we've hidden.

✶ *The Wall as the Shadow*

The poem begins with a dream—bright and full of promise—but as he grows older, a "wall rose between me and my dream." That wall represents the internal and external barriers we face as we mature. In shadow work, we often confront those exact internalized walls: pain, fear, shame, and belief systems that block our light and bury our authentic self.

✶ *Darkness and Light*

Hughes writes,

> "The wall shadowed me!
> The shadow."

Here, shadow is not just the absence of light, but a metaphor for the loss of clarity, purpose, and self. This mirrors the Jungian idea of the shadow self—a part of us that grows in silence when denied, when our truths are suppressed or buried by life's conditioning and pain.

✶ *Breaking Through*

The poem doesn't end in defeat. Instead, the speaker rises with strength:

"I am black and I am beautiful...
I will smash this night,
I will break this shadow."

This moment is the integration of the shadow—naming the pain, reclaiming the power, and choosing to move forward. It's an act of transformation and reclaiming selfhood, exactly what shadow growth seeks to initiate.

✶ *Collective and Personal Relevance*

While Hughes speaks specifically to racial injustice and the crushing weight of systemic oppression, his message also resonates with any journey through internal suppression. The dream deferred, the inner light darkened by outer forces, and the ultimate act of reclaiming power are all aligned with shadow healing.

Before You Write: A Shadow Reflection Activity

In the next section you will be asked to create your own poem inspired by Langston Hughes' "As I Grew Older" poem. His poem offers a powerful, poetic glimpse into the pain of lost dreams and the long road to reclaiming identity and purpose. Though rooted in his personal experience, his words echo something deeply human—a universal encounter with the inner shadows we all face.

Before writing your own poem inspired by Hughes' journey, take time to reflect on these prompts. Each set corresponds to a section of the poem, inviting you to see how your own story may mirror the emotional arc of his. Through this lens, you'll begin to recognize shadow not just as pain—but as the place where your strength, truth, and light begin to rise.

✶ *SECTION 1: The Dream (Hope, Origin, Light)*

"It was a long time ago.
I have almost forgotten my dream..."

☾ What was a dream or version of yourself that once felt vivid and possible?

☾ At what point did you begin to lose sight of that dream, and why?

☾ How do you think your early hopes were shaped by others' expectations or limitations?

☾ What does your "sun" represent—the thing that gave you life or clarity before shadows appeared?

☾ If you could speak to your younger self before they lost that vision, what would you say?

✶ *SECTION 2: The Wall (Obstacles, Suppression, Internalization)*

"And then the wall rose...
Only the wall.
Only the shadow."

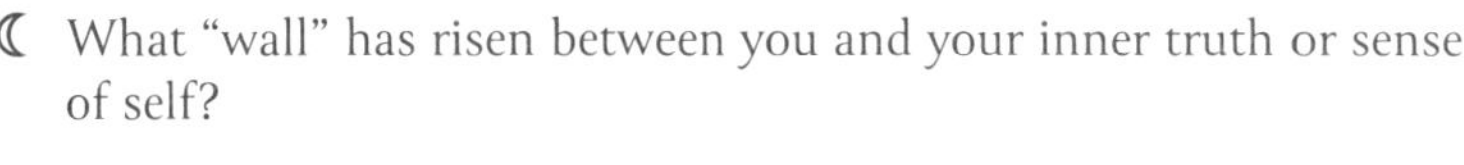

☾ What "wall" has risen between you and your inner truth or sense of self?

☾ Did this wall form slowly, or did it appear all at once? What triggered it?

☾ Whose voices or influences do you believe helped build this wall?

☾ How has this wall shaped the way you see yourself and what you think you deserve?

☾ What emotion lies behind the wall—anger, grief, fear, guilt? Name it.

✶ *SECTION 3: The Shadow (Disconnection, Silence, Hiding)*

"I lie down in the shadow...
No longer the light of my dream before me."

☾ When have you felt invisible, ignored, or buried beneath something larger than yourself?

☾ What part of yourself have you had to hide or silence in order to survive or be accepted?

☾ When did you begin to see your shadow as something to fear instead of understand?

☾ How does it feel to admit what you've lost because of this shadow?

☾ In what ways do you still lie in the shadow—what haven't you reclaimed yet?

✶ *SECTION 4: The Rising (Reclaiming, Power, Transformation)*

"Break through the wall!
To smash this night,
To break this shadow
Into a thousand lights of sun..."

☾ What inner strength or truth is beginning to break through your personal wall?

☾ How have you used your pain as a tool for growth or insight?

☾ What would it look like to fully embrace your shadow, and let it guide you into light?

☾ What do you dream of reclaiming now—whether it's identity, purpose, or joy?

☾ What would "a thousand lights of sun" mean in your life today?

Create Your Own Shadow Poem

Take inspiration from Langston Hughes' "As I Grew Older" and explore the layers of your own shadow. Reflect on the internal struggles you face—those hidden parts of yourself that weigh heavily, linger quietly, or rise in resistance. Use your poem to highlight what you wrestle with, how it makes you feel, and how growth is still possible within the struggle.

Let this be your rising—like a phoenix from the ashes. Allow your words to transform pain into understanding, resistance into reclamation. Shift your perspective on the darkest parts of yourself, and move toward embracing your whole being.

Your poem should come full circle: beginning with the shadow, moving through the conflict, and closing with a sense of self-acceptance, strength, or clarity.

A Shadow Growth Manifesto

A quiet declaration for the self you've met and the self you're still becoming.

I am not afraid of my depth.
I honor what I've hidden, not as weakness, but as wisdom.
I see my pain not as a burden,
but as a bridge to truth.
What I once buried, I now carry with reverence.
My past has shaped me—
but it does not confine me.

I am both the light and the dark,
the breaking and the mending,
the question and the answer.

I will walk forward not as someone fixed,
but as someone free.

✶ *Your Closing Call: Make It Yours*

Take this manifesto and personalize it on the following page.
Change the wording. Add to it. Rewrite it in your voice.
Then sign it—date it—claim it.
This is your declaration of integration.
A reminder that shadow growth was never about becoming someone else—
but about returning to who you already are.

Your Shadow Growth Manifesto

Signed: ______________________ *Date:* ____/____/____

★ *Carry a Reminder*

Write your personalized version of the manifesto on a separate piece of paper or a notecard. Keep it somewhere sacred—by your bed, in a wallet, tucked in a book. Every time you forget who you are, read it again. Whisper it. Breathe it in. Begin again.

*"The shadow
is where
your pain hides,
but also
where your
voice waits."*

– Nayyirah Waheed

Evaluate Your Journey...

☾ What surprised you most about your shadow?

☾ How did your understanding of Carl Jung's shadow theory evolve from the beginning to now?

☾ Which technique felt most natural to you, and why do you think it resonated?

☾ Describe a moment during this process when something within you shifted. What caused that shift?

☾ What protective patterns or armor did you notice yourself shedding, and what has it revealed?

☾ What emotions were the hardest to face? How did you move through them?

☾ In what ways have your relationships changed as a result of this journey—either with others or with yourself?

☾ What version of yourself are you leaving behind, and what are you taking with you?

☾ If your shadow could speak to you now, what would it say? And how would you respond?

You are me
and I am you

☾ Which archetypes did you most identify with, and how do you now see them in your day-to-day life?

☾ What are three beliefs you used to hold about yourself that no longer feel true?

☾ How did it feel to connect with your inner child? What messages came forward from that part of you?

☾ Where in your body did you carry suppressed emotions—and how has that awareness changed how you care for yourself?

☾ What was the hardest chapter or exercise for you, and what did it reveal?

☾ How do you now define growth?

☾ Write a letter to your former self at the beginning of this journey. What would you want them to know?

☾ What new boundaries, truths, or rituals will you carry forward as a result of this work?

☾ If you had to describe this experience in one metaphor or image, what would it be—and why?

☾ What does wholeness mean to you now? Has that definition changed?

☾ How will you continue tending to your shadow in everyday life, outside of these pages?

"The cave you fear to enter holds the treasure you seek."

– Joseph Campbell

A JOURNEY EMBRACED: Reflecting on Your Path of Discovery

As you come to the end of this journal, take a moment to appreciate the incredible journey you've embarked upon. Each page you've filled is a testament to your courage, curiosity, and commitment to understanding and nurturing yourself. You've explored the depths of your emotions, faced your fears, celebrated your strengths, and learned to navigate the intricate landscapes of your inner world.

This isn't just a journal; it's a mosaic of your growth, a collection of insights and reflections that are uniquely yours. You've shown remarkable bravery in delving into the shadows and emerging with a brighter, more profound understanding of who you are. Each word you've written is a step on the path to a more authentic and empowered self.

Remember, the journey of self-discovery doesn't end here. Each day is an opportunity to continue learning, growing, and embracing the full spectrum of your being. Carry the insights and strategies you've gathered in these pages with you as you move forward. Let them be your guide and companion as you navigate the beautiful, ever-unfolding journey of your life.

So, as you close this chapter, know that it's not a goodbye but a gentle nod to the ongoing journey ahead. Celebrate how far you've come, and look forward to the paths yet to be explored. You are a remarkable individual, full of depth, strength, and potential. Here's to your continued journey of discovery, growth, and self-love.

With every page you turn, may you find more reasons to understand, more space to grow, and more moments to cherish. Your journey is a beautiful one, and it's all yours.